Finding Your Company's SPIRITUAL PURPOSE

By

Allen C. Liles

Finding Your Company's SPIRITUAL PURPOSE

By

Allen C. Liles

Published By
Positive Imaging, LLC
bill@positive-imaging.com

ISBN   9781951776534

This book is dedicated to
anyone who has ever worked
for a "company" or "corporation"
Thank you for your service

Contents

Introduction

This book required two lifetimes before it could be written. The first lifetime was spent in the business world as a corporate PR executive for a household name company. The second lifetime featured three decades as an ordained non-denominational minister. Had not both careers dovetailed, I could not bring you this unique perspective that might make a difference for your organization—and the world. Both my careers had more in common than I could have ever expected. I hope you will find something here that will add even more to your company, corporation, LLC, or partnership's reputation and story.

Every successful company has a reason to exist. It has identified a product or service that provides a needed benefit to current and potential customers. The best companies have found a way to keep delivering on that promise. Many corporate success stories have spanned multiple generations. Yet, the history of business failures is legion. Then there are the in-between companies who experienced profitability, even for many decades, before ending up forgotten and bankrupt. Unexpected change happens to companies as it does to individuals. Unless a corpo-

ration possesses strong underpinnings and a
willingness to embrace new ways of doing business, it might be here today and gone tomorrow.
I also believe there is another factor that can
influence a company's longevity. Does the organization have a spiritual purpose for its existence? If it can identify and fulfill the inner
needs of its employees, clients or customers,
that might be the secret ingredient that deter-
mines long-term success or failure. Every corporation has a "culture." It is the sum of everybody
ever associated with the company—its history
and its people. Does the "culture" reflect integrity and spiritual purpose? Who were the founders? What drove them? Are they still around?
Some part of them probably remains even if
their physical presence is gone. Were the past
officers and employees tuned into issues such as
honesty and integrity? What about today? Some
things rarely ever change. Does purpose,
accountability and a service mentality run
through the company today? Does it possess an
identifiable spiritual purpose or "cause"? Does it
still have an important place in the lives of its
customers? The spiritual component of a company or organization may seem like an obscure
and unrelated factor. However, I believe it
might be the elusive x-factor that makes the difference between corporate success and failure.

I served as the public relations officer for a
major American company (7-Eleven Stores). I
was present for more than 20 years (1967-1987)
as it soared from $2 billion to $9 billion in revenues and from 2000 to 7000 7-Eleven Stores.

When I retired to pursue a career in the ministry, it had become the sixth most admired retailer in the entire country (according to Fortune Magazine). I have now served as an ordained minister for the past three-plus decades. Looking back at my two careers, I am amazed how spiritual principles can also impact corporate success. They are more related than you think. Finding your company or organization's spiritual purpose could be the key to staying on the top of the business mountain. Identifying your "cause for being" can bring profitability and fulfillment far beyond anything that you now imagine.

Rev. Allen C. Liles

Temple, Texas

April 2021

1

The Phone Call That Changed Everything

One day in late 1975, my secretary stuck her head inside my office door at The Southland Corporation in Dallas, Texas. "The Chairman is on the phone for you," she told me. I had been public relations manager for Southland and its 6000 7-Eleven Stores for only one year. Prior to moving over to PR, I had spent seven years with the company's prize-winning in-house ad agency. It was the stellar creative group that invented Slurpee, named the Big Gulp and conceived the iconic "OH THANK HEAVEN FOR 7-ELEVEN" ad campaign. Our leader was Bob Stanford, a legitimate advertising legend. The agency's writers included whizzes like Don Coburn, who later wrote a Pulitzer Prize winning play "The Gin Game" and Dan McCurdy, a multi-talented writer and performer.

Southland's chairman was John P. Thompson. His father, Joe C. Thompson, Jr. had founded Southland Ice Company in 1927. Its little Dallas ice houses soon began selling bread, eggs and milk. That was the beginning of the convenience store industry, one of the most incredible success stories in corporate history. Virtually every block in America now boasts a combination gasoline/grocery store. There are more than 150,000 such stores today in the United States alone. Worldwide, there are now more than 70,000 7-Eleven Stores.

At any rate, the Chairman had a request. Southland had just completed its annual fund-raising drive for the Dallas United Way campaign. Our company had collected $975,000. That was no small sum. "We are planning to present the check to United Way tomorrow in my office," John told me. "Could you arrange some media coverage?" he asked. I dutifully contacted our friends with the two daily newspapers and the three TV network affiliates. I even called several radio stations, some of which we were a major advertiser. At the appointed time for the presentation, not one media outlet showed up. I was embarrassed. When I queried a few people about their lack of interest, I was told, "Well, Texas Instruments presented a check to United Way yesterday for $1,250,000. That is where we went. Sorry." Of course, the TI donation was more newsworthy. I could not argue with that reasoning.

However, being shut out by the local media taught me an important lesson. If our company was going to donate a significant amount of money to a charitable cause, we needed to get some recognition for our efforts. At that moment, I became determined to find a way to accomplish that win-win goal for the company. I recalled watching the Jerry Lewis Labor Day Telethon for the Muscular Dystrophy Association (MDA). I remembered Jerry hosting the show and calling various corporate sponsors up to recognize their gifts. It seemed to me that McDonald's was on every couple of hours to bestow another big check. Handing someone a donation publicly seemed an excellent way to at least garner some positive recognition.

I called the local MDA office and they seemed interested in exploring the possibility of 7-Eleven becoming a corporate sponsor. One of their folks mentioned that the Telethon was on for 21 ½ straight hours. That dovetailed with our store's 24/7 operations. The Dallas MDA district people contacted their higher-ups in New York and received a positive response.

"How many stores do you have in Dallas?" a local MDA manager asked me. "I wasn't thinking about just doing it in Dallas," I told her. "Well, how many stores would be involved?" she asked. I replied that we had 6,000 7-Eleven Stores nationally. "How many customers do you all serve?" she inquired. "We average nearly 1,000 customers per day," I answered, "So, I guess that's about six million every day." There was a definite pause on the other end of the telephone. "So, people watching the Telethon could drop by the store and donate in person if they wanted to do so," the MDA person mused.

"Yep," I assured her. "Let me get back to you," she said, "But we are definitely interested."

I discussed the call with Jim Shaughnessy, one of my associates in Southland's PR department. Jim immediately said, "Why don't we just fly out to L. A. and run it by Jerry Lewis in person?" At that moment, the idea seemed a bit presumptuous. However, when MDA called back the next day with an extremely positive response about pursuing a tie-in, I broached the possibility. The Dallas folks offered to check it out with both MDA HQ and The Man himself. The following day, we heard back that a meeting with Jerry was doable. The next week Shaughnessy and I were headed out for California on a Southland jet to meet with the comedian at his office in Century City.

Jerry welcomed us in a friendly, but sort of a non-committal and even skeptical way. He was nice enough and mentioned that he was familiar with the 24-hour 7-Elevens in Las Vegas. However, he quickly reminded us that many potential corporate sponsors were interested in getting exposure on the Telethon. "We have a minimum," he told us firmly, "We're talking about a couple of hundred thousand dollars at least and maybe more." Jim asked him about the McDonald's contribution at the last (1975) Telethon. "They are our biggest corporate sponsor," Jerry said, "Last year they raised over $2 million." I think Jim and I both gulped a bit at the figure. When I had cleared our trip to California with John and Jere Thompson, Southland's chairman and president, respectively, they had asked how much of a dollar commitment we would need to make. "Oh, I really don't know," I hedged, "Maybe $300,000." Jere had just smiled and said, "I know we can do a lot better than that, but don't quote them a figure."

Jerry Lewis had one other hesitation. "I don't know," he frowned, "The 7-Up people are one of our best sponsors. The two names (7-Up and 7-Eleven) are almost identical. I would have to call them first to see what they thought about it." I had done some research about MDA's various corporate sponsors. I already knew of the MDA/ 7-Up connection. I had called one of the 7-Eleven marketing people and asked him "How much 7-Up do we sell at our stores?" He told me, "I can't give you an exact figure, but no other retail store in America sells as much 7-Up as 7-Eleven." I felt confident in urging Jerry to make the call to 7-Up. He did talk to the people in St. Louis after we left his office. They gave him an enthusiastic thumbs-up for 7-Eleven to come on board as an MDA sponsor.

Things were starting to fall into place. However, timing was a problem. Our meeting with Jerry Lewis took place on March 1,1976, only six months before the Labor Day Telethon. I also did not have a final OK from my Southland bosses to proceed. Jim and I went back and met again with Jerry the next day. By this time, he had spoken to a couple of other corporate sponsors (but not McDonald's). Everyone was supportive of 7-Eleven's potential involvement. The comedian seemed intrigued by the synergy between MDA and 7-Eleven as a drop-off point for contributions during the Telethon itself. "How can we move this forward?", he asked. I give Jim Shaughnessy full credit for piping up and saying: "Why don't you fly back with us on the company plane and we can all talk to the Thompsons about it in person." Jerry did not bat an eye. "Give me 24 hours and I can do it," he told us, "But can the plane bring me back to L. A. afterward?" Jim and I got on the phone to Dallas and we were able to arrange everything, including the appointment with the Thompson brothers and the turnaround on the corporate jet. I have learned that when things are meant to be, they fall into place.

Jim and I did have one other potential problem and it could be a deal-killer. We had both worked for Bob Stanford, Southland's iconic advertising manager. Besides being a creative genius, Bob had been an early Dallas TV personality before moving over to do advertising in the corporate world. He was responsible for coming up with a name for 7-Eleven's icy-type drink. "People tend to slurp it," he told us at a staff meeting one day. Hence, the name Slurpee was born. How many Slurpees have been sold worldwide? If you guessed "billions", you would not be far wrong.

At any rate, I had mentioned to Stanford earlier that we were planning to meet with Jerry Lewis about a relationship between 7-Eleven and MDA. "Oh no," he frowned, "I can't stand Jerry's kind of comedy. He is much too slapstick for me. Besides, he is all washed up. Only the French people still like him. I cannot imagine why anybody would pay money to see one of his shows." Jim and I had checked on Jerry Lewis' popularity, because we also thought his glory days might be behind him. We were both surprised to learn that he still had considerable exposure outside of the Labor Day Telethon. Jerry performed several times a year in Las Vegas. He also had tour dates in the U. S, and various appearances in countries around the world. Yes, The French still never missed a year inviting him to perform in their country. Jerry Lewis movies like "The Nutty Professor", his rubbery face, high pitched voice and slapstick "Hey Lady" antics were still popular with many people. His incredible charity work for MDA at the Telethon only enhanced his reputation.

At any rate, Bob Stanford still did not care for him. And, he had been invited by the Thompson brothers to attend the meeting with Jerry. Shaughnessy and I explained the situation to Lewis on the plane trip from L. A. to Dallas. He just shrugged and did not respond. We arrived in Southland's private hangar at Love Field and were picked up for the 15-minute ride ride over to the corporate office on Haskell Avenue. The three of us (Jerry, Shaughnessy and me) all boarded an elevator in our lobby that would take us to an executive meeting room on the top floor. What happened next was a true God thing. The elevator stopped on the sixth floor. The door opened and Bob Stanford got on. I quickly said "Jerry, this is Bob Stanford, South-land's advertising manager." Jerry did not hesi-tate. He grabbed Bob in a big bear hug and started dancing a jig with him. "The great Bob Stanford!" Lewis yelled out in his funny voice, immediately charming the doubting Texan. By the time we arrived on the top floor, Bob and Jerry were best friends. For the ensuing 20-year association between MDA and 7-Eleven, that never changed. The Thompson brothers and Jerry Lewis also began a long and personal friendship. If you ever watched the Telethon between 1976-1995, you might remember the two Thompson brothers (and other 7-Eleven executives) presenting the entertainer with sev-eral large checks during the 21 ½ hour event. Over the two decades of involvement, our com-pany raised nearly $100 million for "Jerry's Kids". Our "Keep the Change" program that first year raised over $3 million for MDA and vaulted us ahead of McDonald's (and everybody else) as the top corporate sponsor. The tie-in was an incredible win-win for everybody. Did 7-Eleven receive the desired recognition for our contributions? Absolutely! Did the annual cam-paign change our company for the better? With-out a doubt! In 1978, the Public Relations Society of America awarded Southland their prestigious Silver Anvil Award. They called the 7-Eleven/MDA campaign the best community relations program that year in the entire coun-try. All of it happened because we were unable to score some local news coverage for a nearly $1 million donation to the United Way. By the way, we still continued that long-time relation-ship too.

I believe something else was also at work in this "feel good" story. It was a perfect spiritual match. The Labor Day Telethon and our all-night 7-Eleven Stores were made for each other. Someone could be watching TV, see the Tele-thon and then decide to stop by a 7-Eleven Store to drop some money into the collection jar.

What about your beloved company? Is there a golden relationship out there just waiting to happen? If so, how do you find it? I believe that, as in many human love matches, there is the perfect someone out there for everybody. If you can manage to connect your organization with the right "cause", it could change everything for the better. It might affect you, your employees and every company stakeholder in a key place—your heart. I guarantee the rewards will be worth the effort for everyone involved.

2

Why Does Your Company Need A Spiritual Purpose?

I see that your stock price may have tripled in the past two years. Your market share is riding a rocket ship to the outer reaches of product stardom. Revenues and profits are surging. Everywhere you go, people are congratulating you for your company's success. So why would you want to dig around in such an esoteric area as finding a spiritual purpose for your company's existence? Here are four practical reasons:

(1) A spiritual purpose can be an unchanging positive when market turbulence erupts.

(2) A bonding of the spiritual among employees, franchisees, vendors, local communities and government entities protects the company from economic, political and cultural blips.

(3) Steeping your company in divine purpose can help mitigate public relations prob-lems and outright disasters.

(4) Claiming the higher ground of a "cause" helps recruit like-minded employees and/or franchisees that value integrity and spiritual purpose.

I can visualize the smart, practical and capa-ble businessmen and women that populate your successful company snorting at this "touchy-feely" list of practical outcomes. I hear and understand their derisive laughter. You are already working hard. Why do you need another program to worry about? Let me share a relevant story with you.

In the 1980s, a company I know well was faced with a business debacle. A couple of rogue division managers in a large North-eastern state were accused of offering a direct bribe to a local city councilman. Money was promised in exchange for liquor licenses. The state attorney's office got involved and there was talk of slapping the company with a RICO (Racketeering) charge. If the com-pany was found guilty, it would suddenly become the equivalent of a convicted felon. The upshot of this status: the prized licenses to sell beer, wine and liquor in a number of states would be pulled. Losing several hun-dred million dollars in sales was a real possi-bility. The well-being of the entire corporation was in real jeopardy. This company's gold-plated attorneys mounted a twin defense: (1) The two rogue managers were an exception and not representative of the company's long-standing anti-corruption policies and (2) The corporation had worked hard to establish and nurture a record as an excellent community citizen. In fact, the Fortune 500 rankings had just designated it as the sixth more admired retailer in the entire U. S. In this case, everybody knew that being convicted would have major negative fallout for many worthy causes. In the end, the company pleaded guilty to a lesser charge that did not carry a felony classification. A real disaster was averted. The company's line operators, who had often questioned the "touchy-feely" programs, were grateful that a positive corporate reputation existed when needed.

Let us take a closer look at the four practical reasons to discover your company's spiritual purpose:

(1) A spiritual purpose can be an unchanging constant when market turbulence erupts. All markets fluctuate. Few stock indices end the day with averages basically unchanged. During the trading hours themselves, there can be many ups and downs. A true spiritual purpose never changes because God never changes. Spirit always remains the same---sacred and eternal. An individual can believe in a wishy-washy God, but it is simply untrue.

God created each one of us. Nothing we can ever do, say or be will ever cause our Creator to love us any less. We are God's blessed children in whom He is well pleased. If you can truthfully identify the spiritual reason for your organization's existence, that too will never change. Now, God also understands that people are human beings. They can make free will decisions that may not turn out well. Exceptionally negative choices could even threaten your company's well-being. Making bad business decisions is a part of the free market system. But the original spiritual reason for your existence should never change. The market for your product or services can be affected by many things, but your true spiritual purpose should stay constant. Managements and governments arrive with new faces and priorities, markets emerge or decline, and the overall economy fluctuates from year to year. However, your real reason for being in business should remain above material considerations.

(2) A bonding of business and the spiritual with employees, franchisees, vendors and local communities and governments can help protect companies from economic, political and cultural stress fractures. We live in contentious times, fraught with

unexpected dangers. Negativity abounds.
Your corporation may be riding high one
day and destroyed by social media the
next. It happens almost every day. Even
the best organization can find itself in hot
water. Human beings make mistakes.
They say foolish things in public. Bad
business decisions can occur anytime.
Your company's actions may result in
legal challenges, as previously described
or surface in some lesser form. Trust me.
When trouble arrives, you will need every
positive arrow in your company's quiver.

(3) Steeping your corporation in divine purpose can mitigate long-term negative consequences. Some crises pass quickly,
without lasting fallout. Others linger for
years before finally dissipating. The most
serious debacles expose weaknesses that
metastasize and kill even the most un-
touchable companies. I believe a strong
spiritual foundation acts like a bolstered
immune system for any temporarily sick
company. It can become the unseen anti-
biotic that restores the organization back
to wholeness. Spirituality defies scientific
measurement. But most people can recognize the divine when it intrudes upon
their five senses. Healing miracles can
happen for companies just like they do for
people. Many companies have come back

from the corporate graveyard. Having a spiritual component in place when trouble strikes is like getting yourself double-vaccinated before the pandemic hits.

(4) Claiming and promoting your company's good deeds should help in attracting like-minded executives, managers, employees, franchisees and even vendors who value integrity, honesty and spiritual purpose. Believe it or not, talented individuals do exist that are inspired by such things. Attraction is even stronger than promotion. If a company is truly walking the walk, the right kind of people will find you. Every single employee is a living and breathing advertisement for the company. The owners and or executive officers provide the ultimate template for the organization. The corporate officers always reflect the company's true standards. Every new hire carries his or her own impressions of a company into the employer-employee relationship. It is hard for a dishonest or corrupt corporation to remain undetected over time. It will turn off far more folks that it turns on.

A bad reputation ripples outward much more than you think.

We will continue reviewing the benefits of a spiritual purpose as we move forward but I want to first share another situation

I experienced during my time at 7-Eleven. It not only presented a major PR problem. It was a matter of life and death.

3

7-Eleven: A Dangerous Place To Work

In the late 1970s, 7-Eleven (and other convenience stores) were viewed as an unsafe place to work. Yet our sales and profits continued to grow. Southland's stock price was on a steady and upward climb. We were expanding into new markets, including foreign countries. We were moving to become a major gasoline retailer. The future looked bright, except for one major area. We were beginning to have trouble hiring employees to work in our 7-Eleven stores. Of course, without the store people there would be no company. For some reason, many who were hired for a clerk's job ended up backing out. When they informed family and friends of their new job, their reaction was anything but positive. In some cases, parents even forbade their son or daughter from working at 7-Eleven. The company did some research. It was a widespread problem across the entire convenience store industry. It could be summed up in two words: personal safety. Many prospective employees succumbed to pressure from loved ones not to take the risk. They did not want their husband, wife, son or daughter robbed, injured or killed during a hold-up. Late night comedians were doing nightly jokes about the number of armed robberies at 7-Eleven. But it was not a funny matter, especially for the operations managers, employees and franchises. Were the perceptions real? How bad was the problem anyway?

It was bad. Having one employee murdered was unacceptable. But, in 1978, 7-Eleven had 12 employees and franchisees killed during a hold-up while on duty in a store. Our 7,000 stores experienced nearly 5,000 robberies and burglaries. That is almost a robbery per year in every store. We had one ill-fated store in Houston that experienced 32 armed robberies in one calendar year. Security guards were hired, but nothing worked. Finally, management just gave up and closed the store. There was no measuring the trauma and collateral damage to everyone involved. Plus, that was one less neighborhood served by 7-Eleven. Then another issue began surfacing. Customers were even staying away from the stores. They did not want to get in the middle of a shootout during a robbery. We had much more than a personnel problem. From both a human and business standpoint, something had to be done. The company had no choice.

Everybody got involved in trying to solve the problem. We put our PR heads together with the top 7-Eleven operations folks and brainstormed

different approaches. Law enforcement participated in the discussions. 7-Eleven holdups were
a big problem for police too. In the interviews
that authorities did with the robbers, some
interesting facts emerged. The crooks were
expecting a take of around $500 per robbery. In
some cases, they were getting that and much
more. The bad guys loved the same thing about
the little stores that customers craved: Quick,
fast and in and out service. Risk-reward was
working in favor of the crooks. The first thing
that needed attention was to reduce the payoff
for the robber. The operations managers devised
a new type of super-lock safe where money could
be deposited every hour or even every few minutes. The safe was not accessible to the regular
clerks after the money was dropped. As a result,
the total amount of cash available in the regis-
ter, if all instructions were followed, would drop
to $50 or less. That represented a much bigger
risk for any armed robber. Most jail sentences
for this type of felony were running about five
years. Getting caught and convicted for an average of ten bucks a year did not make sense in
most criminal minds. I recall a TV series back in
the day about "Stupid Criminals". Of course,
more than a few felons deserve that reputation.
However, do not ever underestimate the criminal mind. Many are much smarter and more
careful than you might think. For the most part,
unless they are desperate or on drugs, they
operate with a sophisticated model. Most criminals weigh the odds against getting caught. If
they even thought about robbing a 7-Eleven

store, a measly payoff of fifty bucks did not make sense.

Everyone hoped the new drop safe would eventually be a deterrent for the crooks. They watch TV and keep up with the news too. Once word got around that hitting a 7-Eleven Store was not a big payoff anymore, hopefully they would now think twice. However, the overall public perception of 7-Eleven as a crime magnet would be harder to overcome. We had three major groups to "target" (so to speak) with our Robbery Prevention Program. One was our customers who wanted a safe shopping experience. Another was our prospective employees and franchisees. The third "public" we needed to reach was the criminal community itself. The quicker the crooks learned of the new money-drop policy, the more protected our clerks would be. Then, as robberies declined, the public's perception would hopefully change. Every 7-Eleven store quickly displayed a prominent decal near the front door that advised both customers and would-be criminals of the $50 maximum in the register. Over In PR, we searched for a creative way to grab some media attention for our new anti-crime program. Just proclaiming that we were lowering the cash in the register would be newsworthy for a while. However, it had limited appeal over the long term as a news story.

We decided to find a credible spokesperson to explain the program. We needed someone that could not only spread the message, but also attract media attention. Just hiring an actor to

tout the program did not seem innovative
enough. Somebody recalled a research project
initiated by our San Diego 7-Eleven management people. They had hooked up with the
Western Behavioral Science Institute in La
Jolla, CA. WBSI was doing credible research on
various aspects of crime. It was run by a brilliant PhD and social scientist named Waymon
"Bud" Crow. Dr. Crow was a well-regarded long-
time associate of an American psychological
trail blazer—Dr. Carl Rogers. Rogers founded
the humanistic ("person- centered") approach to
psychotherapy that is still used today. Bud
Crow was far more than your typical "shrink".
He understood business. He was also a guy who
regularly shopped at the 7-Eleven Stores in
southern California. He knew some of the franchisees and store employees personally. Bud
was ably complemented in his work by his
equally brilliant and talented wife Rosemary
Erickson. Together Bud and Rosemary had built
WBSI into one of the nation's premier social
behavior research groups. They approached 7-
Eleven's robbery prevention problem with
knowledge, wisdom, intellect, passion and science. WBSI did several interesting things,
including forming a panel of armed robbers. A
couple of them had robbed one or more of our
stores. One of these unsavory "gentlemen" was a
recidivist armed robber named Ray Johnson. He
was the ultimate character besides being a
career criminal. Although being incarcerated 25
of his 47 years, Ray J had been married nine
times. At one point in his later life, seven of

Ray's former wives held a formal reunion in his honor. At some point, Johnny Carson read about Ray's nine ex-spouses and invited him to appear on the TONIGHT SHOW. Before Johnny's retirement in 1992, Ray appeared on the show 30 times and had been bumped an equal number of times as the final guest of the evening. Carson loved Ray's funny stories about prison life and the peculiarities of the criminal mind. However, Ray Johnson was no wannabee. He was the real deal. Ray was one of the few inmates in history who had ever escaped from Folsom Prison. The authorities quickly caught up with Ray and his two buddies after the threesome refused to kill a witness to their escape. During his crime sprees, Ray had never physically harmed anyone. After his release from prison, he spent the last 20 years of his life helping companies like 7-Eleven with their crime prevention challenges. His self-written autobiography "Too Dangerous to Be At Large" was a best seller. A made for TV movie entitled "Dangerous Company" was produced about his life. Ray was played by Beau Bridges. In the 1980s, he received a full pardon from California governor Jerry Brown. Our company was incredibly fortunate to find Ray Johnson. Things like that tend to fall into place when a legitimate spiritual purpose exists. Protecting employees, franchisees and customers from crime was a true spiritual endeavor.

Ray was a fabulous spokesperson for 7-Eleven's Robbery Prevention Program. The media loved to interview him. To say that he was a colorful

character understates the obvious. I recall having dinner at "The Sign of the Dove" restaurant
in New York City one night with Ray and two of
my Southland associates. Suddenly, Ray J
looked up and saw a familiar figure standing at
the bar. "That's Tony Bennett!" Ray shouted, "I
met him in the Green Room at the Carson
Show. Wait here." Whereupon Ray sped to the
bar, grabbed the famous singer and brought him
over to meet his 7-Eleven friends. A surprised
Tony was most gracious and even seemed
pleased to see the ex-convict again.

So, how did Ray and the program do in reducing
store robberies? They were down a full 25% during the first year and another 50% over the next
three years. Before Ray and the new safes
appeared on the scene, our robberies had been
growing by 15% every year. One sheriff in
Southern California predicted that every 7-
Eleven store in the nation would be robbed at
least once a year. That was an outcome nobody
wanted. Had the tide not been reversed, the
company would have suffered grave damage to
its reputation and bottom line. That does not
include the most important thing: the safety of
our store people and customers.

The tragic death of any 7-Eleven clerk or franchisee was a wrenching and terrible event. I
recall attending a funeral in Dallas for a store
employee named April Tufts. Her tragic death
was senseless. She had complied with the robber's demands (which we always told the clerks
to do) and he had still taken her life. We also

discovered that some foreign-born franchisees on the West Coast and East Coast declined to surrender the store's money, even at gunpoint. It represented a loss of face in their culture. Some of these tough store people fought gallantly with the robbers and even subdued many of the surprised crooks. We also had a policy of no guns in the store. Ray Johnson was instrumental in convincing our people that guns encourage violence rather than prevent it. Money can be replaced. Ray Johnson did many in-person programs for our employees and franchisees, always trying to help them understand the crime from an armed robber's perspective. I am sure this ex-crook, turned good guy, saved the lives of many 7-Eleven clerks and franchisees. He had become a crime-fighting legend before he passed in 1989 at the age of 62. No word on how many of his ex-wives attended the memorial service. Ray had been married to his lovely wife Joanna for a decade at the time of his death. Bon voyage, Ray J. You were one of the smartest and most honest people I met during my 20 years with the company. You were indeed the real deal. Thank you for your service.

4

Any Successful Company Represents A Reflection Of God's Grace In Action

I know, I know. Your company is successful because of you and your great people. Of course, you did have some outside help and a few good breaks. The market was timed perfectly for your product or service. You had a unique idea and executed it flawlessly. Your marketing and advertising campaigns were killer. Your investors were visionaries. Mainly, you did the difficult work required for any business success. You put in the hours. You were single minded. Your family made the necessary sacrifices. Every little thing fell into place. Now you are reaping the rewards. Your back sometimes gets a tad bruised from all the congratulatory pats. You are in constant demand, publicly and privately. Life is good. What is there to complain about?

When you have the time in your busy schedule, block out about an hour. Find a quiet place where you will not be disturbed. This is your reflection time. But it should not concern the next great ad campaign or whether to hire an Ivy League executive v-p that can share the load. This is the blessed moment in time to truly reflect on how you got here.

Picture the people, places and things who are behind your success. Visualize their faces in the crowd that surrounds you. First, see the proud smiles on your parent's faces. In your case, it is just your dear mother that beams down at you. Unfortunately, you never knew your cop dad. You were a 22 month old toddler when he died in the endless war on law enforcement. You inherited many informal dads from the department. None romantically for your mom, of course, No one could replace your hero dad. But there were numerous "father figures" who stepped up and contributed to your college fund. It put you through a five-star university with no college debt. Your mom did go back to nursing school and became an RN. She worked as an ICU nurse until the pandemic took her. You still remember the many tearful accolades at her memorial service. Most of the people you had never seen before, but they all knew your mother. Say thank you mom, for not abandoning you after your dad passed much too soon. She was a larger than life hero too. There is a lot of both your parents in you.

I see your 8th grade teacher standing behind you. You gave her some hard times. Do you remember the day when you pushed the envelope a little too far and disrespected her? Of course, you do. She called you by your first, middle and last name and demanded that you stand up in front of the entire class. Then, she tore you a new one. "You could be a brilliant student!" she addressed you with coldness and proper contempt, "But you're a lazy, worthless and an arrogant fool. You think you are too cool for school. You look down on your fellow students, especially those who apply themselves. Even if you get lucky and become successful, it will not matter. You can never be humble. I feel sorry for you. Personally, I predict you will not never amount to anything." Do you remember the deafening silence as your classmates just stared at you? After that dressing down, you spent every day trying to prove her wrong. When you walked across the stage as the high school valedictorian, you looked for that crabby teacher in the crowd. You spotted her near the back of the auditorium. She was smiling at you and applauding! She should be mad! You proved her wrong. You just cannot figure out some people. Of course, you still remember the nice note she wrote later congratulating you. "You just needed a kick in the butt," she said. Then, she added: "I expect great things from you."

I also see Frank Johnson, your first boss after college. Frank spent hundreds of extra hours teaching you the ins and outs of your business specialty. You regarded the poor guy as a dinosaur. Although just 15 years your senior, Frank seemed hopelessly outdated in terms of today's technology. You appreciated the extra help he gave you, of course, but wished he would opt for early retirement at 40. You always wondered why he was being so helpful. You would not have possessed the time and patience to mentor anyone. Did you ever wonder what happened to Frank? He never had much of a career after leaving the company. He passed away before he reached 50. Too bad, really.

Let us see who else is in the crowd. There is Brenda, the lady who used to clean your office at work. She always did such a good and careful job. The two of you enjoyed a friendly relation-ship. You enjoyed visiting back and forth until the day she asked you for a personal loan. Bren-da's 10-year-old "special needs" son required an operation. You did not understand the specific reason for the surgery. All you heard was "loan". You mumbled a question as to whether Medic-aid would cover his medical expenses. You assumed Brenda was on welfare Then you made an excuse about having to leave the office early. You never spoke with her again. You made sure you were out of the office on the days she cleaned. But here she stands anyway, right behind you. Why would she be smiling?

Finally, I see three of your former girlfriends, standing with locked arms. That is surprising, as you had made sure they never knew about each other. However, not one of them is smil-ing. Each one of them loved you in her own way. You disappointed them all, walking away when you were needed or reneging on a commitment. Oh well, they certainly received many perks from knowing you. You never forgot a birthday. And those gifts were expensive!

Now, in all fairness, let us switch the group.
These new faces appear much happier. I see
your family of origin, with two intact and long-
married parents. Their pride in you is obvious.
Your three successful siblings openly applaud
you. Several of your high school teachers and
university professors look admiringly in your
direction. A handful of your business associates
and employees also have gathered to honor you
as their leader. I even see some military officers
from your graduating class at the Academy
saluting you. Your beaming wife and smiling
children are by far the proudest of them all.
They are all so happy and grateful that you are
part of their lives. Their hearts overflow with
genuine love and respect for you.

Which group looks the most familiar to you?
Whichever one it may be, they are part of your
past, present and future. Their influence has
shaped who you are and who you will become.
However, there is yet another key element at
work in your life. It cannot be perceived with
any of your five senses. That unseen entity is
God, your Creator. Your spiritual Father placed
every person, place or thing in your life for a
reason. It molded you into the person you are
today. The Creator of the entire universe also
blessed you with a priceless gift—Grace. It was
God's Grace that has enriched your life and the
organization and customers you serve. Do you
really think you made it here all by yourself?
Was it your brains, hard work and determina-
tion alone that won the day? Or did God's amazing Grace play an unseen but crucial role in

your human life? Grace falls at your feet as we speak. You cannot see, touch, smell, taste or feel it. Yet, God's eternal Grace is the real manna from Heaven. Do not wait. Claim your heavenly Grace now. Ask God to bless you on the wonderful but perilous journey that lies ahead. Let me ask you another question. If God is for you in your personal, business and spiritual life, who can be against you? The answer is "nobody". Keep on climbing toward the final rainbow.

Accept the enlightenment that comes with spiritual Grace. Whether you understand it or not, an illumination is taking place in your life. You are being called to your own spiritual destiny. You did not choose God. He chose you to use your talents and influence in a positive way. God wants you to help lift the world higher. Your beloved and successful company could be an important part of that spiritual journey. Many of God's servants, even from Biblical days, were just everyday people chosen to bless humankind. Become open and receptive to what Path may await you. I promise it will never be boring.

Part of your future could be spent on furthering a "cause" greater than yourself or your company. In fact, your corporate success may have opened the way to undertaking this "cause". It might be the real reason why you are here in the first place. Be alert, open and receptive. Big surprises may be in store.

5

Allowing Your Company's History
To Work For You

The Southland Corporation began as a block ice
company in the Oak Cliff section of Dallas, TX
in 1927. Joe C. Thompson, Jr. (who was then 26
years old) and a few of his close friends named
their new enterprise The Southland Ice Company. One day a customer walked into one of the
stores and suggested to the clerk Uncle Johnny
Greene that he start selling bread, eggs and
milk along with the block ice. It was not long
before the convenience store industry was
birthed. Southland changed the name of the
stores to 7-Eleven soon after World War II. The
designation initially referred to its hours of
operation. In the 1960s, customers in Las Vegas
asked that the stores remain open 24 hours, 7
days a week. The name stayed the same but
soon every store was available every hour of the
day and night. People soon learned that, when
they needed something, 7-Eleven was the most
convenient place to get it. During the first year
of opening stores in the Washington, D. C. area,

a massive snowstorm shut down the regular grocery outlets, even in the Virginia and Maryland suburbs. Hungry and thirsty customers flooded into the little 7-Eleven store on the corner. For the first time, people began to understand and appreciate where these neighborhood stores might fit into their daily lives. Soon, mainly through the efforts of Bob Stanford (my first boss at Southland's in-house ad agency), the 7-Eleven store also developed its own unique personality. It became a fun and happening place to go. Bob and Howard W. Greene (his creative cohort) invented Slurpee (with various crazy flavors), Big Gulp, Hot to Go fast foods, and a host of other popular products. Kids, men and later working women loved it. In my first year at the agency in 1967, they came up with some classic Slurpee flavors like "Fulla Bulla", and our Valentine's Day favorite "Kiss Me, you Fool." Bob also developed some funny characters for his award-winning radio commercials. One he christened "Y. Y. Wickey". "Y. Y." was voiced by the supremely talented Frank Harting, the company's first PR Manager and my predecessor in the job. Frank was known as the guy who wrote First Lady Eleanor Roosevelt and invited her to his birthday party one year when he was working in New York City. She showed up, much to everybody's surprise. That began a personal friendship with the Roosevelts that resulted in several visits to the White House when FDR and Eleanor were the long-term occupants.

Southland and 7-Eleven really began to boom
after founder Jodie Thompson, Jr. died in 1961.
There were 400 stores back then, mostly in
Texas and some in Florida. I remember the 7-
Eleven Store near the high school in my hometown of Temple, TX when I was growing up. The
store was located on North 3rd Street and was a
great place to grab a Dr Pepper or Coca-Cola.
August Lange, the long-time store manager,
knew every one of us by name and our parents
as well. Shoplifting was unheard of in those
days. It never crossed anybody's mind. Anyway,
when the elder Mr. Thompson passed, responsibility for running the company fell to the founder's two sons John P. Thompson and Jere W
Thompson. John and Jere were 36 and 31,
respectively. They immediately began to expand
the company. When I joined Southland on May
1, 1967, there were 2.000 stores. When I offi-
cially retired in 1988, there were 9,000 7-Elev-
ens in most states, parts of Canada and a few
foreign countries. 7-Eleven was wildly popular
in places like Japan, where the manager usually
lived above the store. Ito Yokado, a successful
Japanese retailer was our partner there. They
would play a crucial role in Southland's fortunes
in later years. There are now more 70,000 7-
Eleven Stores worldwide, including Japan,
mainland China, Hong Kong, South Korea, Tai-
wan, and Singapore. There are still more than
11,800 stores in North America. You can find us
throughout Europe as well.

Our company also owned a collection of dairies
with regional brand names (like Velda Farms in

Florida, Oak Farms in Texas and Midwest
Farms in Memphis). Southland also purchased
some specialty grocery stores such as Gristede's
in New York City and brands like candy-maker
Barracini. There was still a Southland Ice division, a half-dozen major distribution centers
(later owned by Wal-Mart and then Warren Buffet) and even an auto parts store (Chief). Our
sales in the mid-1980s were nearly $10 billion
annually. During my time at the company, we
never had a down quarter. It was always
onward and upward. Back in 1975, Southland
decided to celebrate its 50th anniversary in
1977. As part of the festivities, I proposed that
we add a company history book to the mix. The
Thompson brothers liked the idea. To hold down
expenditures, they asked if I could author it. I
was happy to do so. I took on the project with
gusto. It turned out to be a terrific thing for me
and, an even better thing for the company, its
officers and employees, franchisees, shareholders, vendors, and simply people who were interested in how 7-Eleven became so popular. At the
time, I made kind of a bold decision. In retro-
spect, I took a real chance. I decided to put my
name on the book as the "author". I now realize
that had the project bombed, I would have been
forever known as the doofus who managed to
screw up the company's history. The entire project took two years to complete: six months to
research, six months to write, six months to
fact-check and edit, and six months to get it
approved and printed. I did most of the work at
night and on weekends. It turned out to be a

"labor of love". There were many times I could feel "The Founder" (Joe C. Thompson, Jr) looking over my shoulder as I pounded away on my little portable electric typewriter. We ended up printing 100,000 copies of the 264-page book. It was titled "OH THANK HEAVEN—THE STORY OF THE SOUTHLAND CORPORATION". You can still find copies for sale today on Amazon.com and Ebay. The book was furnished free to the various company "publics" that we mentioned earlier. We also provided it to the news media. People seemed to find it interesting and enlightening. In the PR Department alone, we were blessed to get back 1,500 letters and cards about the book. Only three responses were negative (this was in the day before social media) and they contained only mild criticism. A couple of folks thought we had spent too much money on producing the book. Actually, it looked more expensive than it was. That is always a good thing. Southland's two great designers, Hans Streich and DeeAnn Steiger did a magnificent job putting it all together. The Kingsport Press in Tennessee did an excellent job printing the book at a very reasonable cost. The Thompson brothers were overwhelmed by the feedback they personally received. Probably my nicest compliment came from Jerry Lewis at the 1977 Labor Day Telethon. He told me: "Well, I read your Oh Thank Heaven book. Now it's not "Gone With the Wind," but for a company history it held my interest."

What did the "OH THANK HEAVEN! history book accomplish for the company: (1) It told a

unique business story about real people building
a trail blazing company while inventing a brand
new retailing concept; (2) It showed the suc-
cesses and failures that populate and humanize
every company's story; (3) It helped our employees, franchisees, vendors, and shareholders to
understand our company's long journey and the
collection of real live human beings who made it
all happen; (4) It provided potential investors
with an overview of the company's strengths
and even possible weaknesses; (5) It had the
potential to attract new employees and franchisees; (6) It gave the company a credible PR and
promotional tool that could be used with the
news media and various other publics; (7) It
offered a public record of people and events that
could be utilized as a historical resource by
present and future generations of management;
(8) It captured recollections from individuals
who would someday disappear from the scene,
along with their memories; (9) It identified and
affirmed the spiritual purpose for the company's
existence, i. e. to offer fast and convenient service when needed and (10) It might help inspire
future generations of entrepreneurs and managers in all sorts of businesses to learn what
shapes success. Of course, the company's history
lives on today via the internet. Whether you
search for 7-Eleven, The Southland Corporation,
John P. Thompson or just convenience stores in
general, there is a good chance that OH THANK
HEAVEN/THE STORY OF THE SOUTHLAND
CORPORATION will pop up as a reference or
resource.

The book also revealed many unexpected truths. For me, one of the biggest revelations was the role customers played in new product develop- ment. Several people in the Washington, D. C. area came up with the idea of putting a coffee maker in the store. 7-Eleven was Starbucks (except for the fancy stuff) before Starbucks. We were selling microwaveable sandwiches before they started making them by hand at many of our fast-food chain restaurants. Virtually all our major retailing ideas came from customers or store people. That might be something for any company to ponder when viewing "headquar- ters" as the fount of all wisdom. Store people and customers always know what the public wants.

Done correctly, with the right priorities, a com- pany history will not be a puff piece or "ain't we all grand" serenade. People like to hear about when the company screwed up and learned something from its mistakes. When 7-Eleven decided to close one of its Fort Worth stores, it put up a hand-crafted store front banner that admitted "OPENED BY MISTAKE". Human beings can identify with failure. It happens to everyone. I also believe that people like to read about the stores and products they personally use. I wonder how many people have trooped up to 7-Eleven in the middle of a snowy night to fetch some aspirin or cough syrup. Maybe you know somebody (perhaps your son or daughter) who stopped by 7-Eleven after a Little League game for a Slurpee. You might remember going into the store for a coffee and donut on the way to work. Almost everyone could conjure up a 7-Eleven story if they thought about it.

I hope you will consider telling your company's story. Every day that you hesitate, an important voice or memory might disappear forever. I promise that somebody, somewhere will benefit from your company's story. You might put your name on that list too. You have earned it.

6

How a Company Physical Helped Me Discover Meditation and Changed My Life Forever

Meditation (also referred to as Mindfulness) can be a healthy, stress-removing factor in balancing the rigors of modern life. Once considered only an ancient Eastern spiritual practice, millions of people now practice the art of meditation. It is a medically proven stress reliever. Meditation can bring down blood pressure, be effective in treating heart disease and in just settling down jangled nerves. As someone who began practicing meditation in 1985 when I was still in corporate world, I can say with certainty it has changed every area of my life for the better. For my health and peace of mind, meditation came along at an opportune moment in my life journey.

In 1986, my last full year at Southland, I went for the executive physical examination required for corporate officers. It was a full day of tests and interviews conducted by the world-renowned Cooper Clinic on Preston Road in Dallas. You have probably heard about "Aerobics". Dr. Kenneth Cooper invented it. Aerobics was originally developed for the NASA space program in the 1960s. Its purpose was to monitor the vital signs of the astronauts being sent into orbit. A former Air Force physician, Dr. Cooper founded The Cooper Institute in 1970. The Cooper name and reputation are the gold standard in evaluating the current state of an executive or corporate manager's physical health. They are also experts in offering a prediction for someone's future health. At the end of a full day of tests, exams and measurements, you sit down with a Cooper doc and get the good or bad news. Predicting your healthy or unhealthy future is the bottom-line purpose of the entire day. I was 49 years old at the time of my Cooper physical. I was not overweight, had never smoked and was a four or five drink per week social drinker. Recreational drugs were never my thing. I did have a lot of personal stress from a recent divorce following a 23-year marriage. I was also having vigorous disagreements with my son about his marijuana use. Then there were the usual stressful goings on at the company. That included managing 35 PR professionals and support staff. Overall, I thought I was in decent shape. I had not been an overnight patient in a hospital since my sophomore year in high school. Perhaps the biggest change in my most recent lifestyle habits did involve being newly single. Without question, I had increased my alcohol intake to maybe seven or eight drinks per week. Still, I took virtually no medications, including for high blood pressure. I did take a pill for my inherited high cholesterol. In addition, I had some significant family history of heart disease and cancer. My dad died from his third heart attack in 1979 at the age of 67. My mother passed in 1969 at 56 from breast cancer. However, my paternal grandfather smoked cigars every day of his adult life and made it to age 93. When I sat down with my assigned Cooper physician at the end of the day, I was reasonably confident about my health situation. I knew the doc had already reviewed my test results and labs. I went into the consult with high expectations of being praised for my sterling condition. The doctor sat back in his chair and asked how I was feeling. Then he leaned forward and visibly frowned. Uh-oh, I thought.

"Fine!" I responded with a broad smile.

"Well, unfortunately, I have some not so good news for you" he said.

"What's that?" I inquired, feeling a sudden apprehension.

"I may as well be honest with you," he told me, "Unless you make a radical change to your current lifestyle, you have a 90% probability of a major cardiac event. It could even be catastrophic. I think we are looking at a heart attack or stroke sooner rather than later. I would say that you might have three years or less before everything catches up with you. You do not have much time to make some big changes. Delay is not an option. If you want to live, that is."

I almost did experience one cardiac event right then as my heart traveled straight up to my throat.

"What's my basic problem?" I asked meekly.

"Well, you have four or five major factors, beginning with your family history. Your father had his first heart attack at the age of 49. That is your age now. His cholesterol was unsustainable, near 500. Yours is in the 380 range and that is with medication. Your father did smoke two packs of cigarettes a day, so that one is in your favor. However, neither you nor your dad saw exercise as a deterrent to heart disease. He was overweight, but not obese. You are 5-7 pounds too heavy. You dine out a lot in traveling for your company. Too much expense account eating is not a good thing for you or anybody. You are a pre diabetic, so all the rich food does not help in that area. However, the biggest problem for you is stress. Yours is off the charts. Stress is cumulative. You have racked up a lot of high stress events this past year, including a divorce and moving to a new residence. You were in a long-term marriage for nearly 23 years. You told one of your counselors that you are now going out with different women three or four times a week. Pursuing new relationships can be a highly stressful activity, especially for a man nearly 50 years old. That is why married people live longer. However, work is by far your biggest stress factor. You were promoted to vice president of public relations three years ago. You are now a corporate officer for the biggest company headquartered in Dallas. You are responsible for their good name throughout the world. To help you in this important job, you are now managing over 35 people. Family history, divorce, high corporate stress and no exercise are setting the stage for a big-time cardiac event. It is almost a given. I just cannot tell you when it will happen. You do not have much time to make big changes. I do not want to "scare you straight", but time is of the essence."

He then sat back in his chair and continued frowning.

I tried to process his diagnosis. I felt disappointed and dismayed. I thought I was handling everything pretty well. Looking back now, I was in total denial about my health situation. Of course, the Cooper doc was spot on about everything. In fact, he might have let me off too easy. Of course, my family history and the divorce I could not change. I did have good intentions when it came to exercise. I had joined a health club the year before. However, I only went twice. I had not darkened the gym door in six months. I thought about walking as an exercise, but never seemed to find the time. Between work, traveling and chasing women, I already had a full schedule. Exercise was far down my list of priorities.

As part of the assessment, the Cooper physician tried to help me understand how alcohol and co-dependency (especially with women) were affecting me. What a revelation that was! Men of my generation were just now learning how to express our "feelings". Our heroes growing up were the strong, silent types like Gary Cooper and John Wayne. It was "yep" and "nope" when it came to handling problems. I had also never dreamed how drinking, family dynamics and daily emotional stress could affect the strongest person, male or female. I do appreciate now that the visit to the Cooper Clinic changed my life. It was as if God had dispatched a guardian angel with a cosmic 2 x 4 and applied it to my forehead. Of course, it took some time for me to get serious about changing my lifestyle. However, allow me to summarize the actions I took between that day in 1986 and where I found myself five years later in 1991.

1. I retired early from Southland at the end of 1986.

2. I quit drinking entirely in 1989. I have now been alcohol free for 32 years.

3. I joined Al-Anon, a 12-step recovery program for families of alcoholics, also in 1989. I still attend approximately three group meetings every week.

4. I found a positive Christian movement (Unity), that is based on the practical teachings of Jesus Christ. In the Unity

principles, I learned to appreciate the concept of an indwelling, loving and caring God.

5. I applied for and was accepted into Unity's Continuing Education Program in 1989 and Religious Studies Program in 1991. I became an ordained Unity minister two years later in 1993.

6. I began a daily exercise program of both walking and the treadmill.

7. I learned the ongoing health and spiritual benefits of daily meditation. God and I meet every morning for prayer and a check-in. I do a lot of listening.

8. I made a commitment to my wonderful wife (Jan Carmen Liles) in 1991. We married in 1994 and became partners in ministry. Jan and I were happily married for nearly 23 years before she passed in 2017. We served various Unity churches after my ordination. I also spent six years at Unity's world headquarters from 1995-2001 as Senior Director for Outreach.

9. Through meditation, I learned how to "Let Go and Let God" direct my life. In communing with God during meditation, I ask only for knowledge of God's will for my life and the power to carry it out.

Wow! if I do say so, that represents a 180 degree change from where I began that day at the Cooper Clinic. Looking back now, it boggles my mind that so much has transpired. All I can say is "Thank you, God."

Of all the things that have transformed my life, meditating every day has been the most meaningful. After becoming an ordained minister, it was also a regular part of my Unity church services. We do a guided meditation every Sunday morning. Congregants look forward to this time in the silence. Over the years, I have observed some truths about "practicing" the Presence of God through meditation. I noticed several inhibitors that deter people from trying meditation as a stress reducer. Some see it as an "Eastern" or "New Age" endeavor. But many people also avoid meditation because of (a) not being sure they are doing it correctly and (b) because their busy minds will not cooperate and become quiet. Regarding the first objection, let me promise you there are no "bad" meditations. At the beginning of my own practice, some of my best times in the silence occurred in the express lane at the supermarket. When I would find myself stuck in the "10 items or less" lane behind somebody with 30-plus items, I would not get mad or become impatient. I would take that opportunity to close my eyes and meditate. It helped a lot. The second objection about not being able to shut down an active mind is understandable. it just requires patience and practice, practice, practice. Some people focus on using a one word "mantra". They just keep repeating "Peace,

peace, peace" over and over or "love, love, love"
until the brain begins to ramp down. When you
commence your meditation practice, try to cut
yourself some slack. Do not be too hard or criti-
cal on yourself. Strive for progress, not perfec-
tion. The spiritual Path is always two steps
forward and one step back. I believe your busy
brain will eventually embrace and cherish the
serenity that comes with meditation. Remember
this Truth: you and God united in Oneness represent a mighty force for good. Becoming connected with your Higher Power offers relief from
stress. I hope you will embrace the benefits of
meditation. As the old Alka-Seltzer commercial
told us many years ago: "Try it. You'll like it."

7

The PR And Spiritual Value Of Sports

During my time in advertising and public relations at The Southland Corporation, I learned how a positive "sports" tie-in could burnish any company's reputation. That fact is still true today. Southland was blessed with many productive sports relationships.

We owned several regional dairies. "Oak Farms" was our brand in Texas. "Velda Farms" in Florida was a Southland dairy. "Midwest Farms", in the Memphis area also displayed the distinctive and colorful fleur-de-lis logo common to our dairy products. Of course, we sold our milk, ice cream and other dairy items at the 7-Eleven Stores. But we also had many other retail customers who valued their relationship with the Southland dairies.

Several of our milk companies had outstanding programs with local and regional sports teams. Oak Farms and the Dallas Cowboys worked together from the team's beginning in the early

1960s. I recall attending a photo shoot with Cowboy quarterback Don Meredith where he held up a dairy carton and urged fans to drink Oak Farms milk. To this day, I remember Meredith's fabulous personality. He began calling me by my first name the moment we shook hands. I also recall having lunch one day with the great (but mostly reticent) Tom Landry. Dallas' Hall-of-Fame coach radiated total purpose and focus. But he clearly regarded making nice with corporate sponsors as a burden. He was polite, but also cut short the lunch with the Southland dairy execs. Coach Landry mentioned something about "getting back to practice." That dedication took him to five Super Bowls.

Velda Farms and the Miami Dolphins were great partners. Our company had a terrific sales manager at the dairy. Russ Nicoll personally knew every Florida retail customer. Russ was especially tight with the Dolphins. I never personally met Don Shula, but Russ and I went to the dog races one afternoon with Dolphins QB Bob Griese. I also met Joe Robbie, the Dolphins owner. I recall him sharing with us that he had a child graduating that year from elementary school, middle school, high school and college. I believe Mr. Robbie had 11 kids and was he ever proud of them all. Velda Farms was fortunate to sponsor the Dolphins during their 17-0 Super Bowl run in 1972.

Midwest Farms in Memphis loved their sports tie-in with the regionally popular St. Louis Cardinals. Again, Southland was blessed with a trio

of terrific sales folks—Jack Gentle, Nick Douzanis and Tom Hill. As a rookie ad account exec
serving Midwest, I made the suggestion to Jack,
Nick and Tom that we offer a baseball "clinic" in
Memphis featuring several Cardinal players. It
almost turned into a disaster. As part of the
program, we scheduled an autograph session
after the clinic. We had booked the stadium of
the local minor league team as the site. We
anticipated that maybe 1,000-2,000 fans might
show up. On the day of the clinic, more than
10,000 people flooded into the stands and out
onto the field itself. After all, who would not
want the opportunity to see and hear from Tim
McCarver, Bob Gibson, Curt Flood and Dal
Maxvill. Our mistake was trying to hold an
autograph session afterwards. It turned into a
mini riot with lots of pushing and shoving. We
had to call in extra security from the Memphis
Police Department to extricate the players
before somebody got hurt. That experience
taught me that a PR tie-in can sometimes be too
successful. I was more careful with my suggestions after that fiasco.

7-Eleven had sports tie-ins as well. In 1980, I
was invited by the Thompson brothers to attend
a lunch in New York City with Peter Uberroth.
Jere Thompson and Mr. Uberroth knew each
other from YPO (Young President's Organization). Peter had been chosen to act as CEO for
the 1984 Olympic games in Los Angeles. He
owned a successful travel agency and knew
many corporate executives. At the time, the
Olympics itself had garnered a negative reputa-

tion for gigantic overspending and leaving host cities with big deficits. Peter Uberroth was determined that would not happen with his games. He launched an all-out blitz of signing up corporate sponsors. Coca-Cola, McDonald's, the Busch breweries and other corporate giants immediately committed millions of dollars to become sponsors. Peter pitched the Thompsons to consider 7-Eleven also becoming involved. The meeting in New York was to discuss that possibility. On the plane ride to the East Coast, I asked if any minimum commitment had been mentioned. Jere said "I hear Coke has already pledged $10 million. I told Peter we could not do anything like that." A thought occurred to me: I asked John and Jere if the Olympic Committee was planning to construct any special venues for the games that did not currently exist. They had not heard of any needs in that area. At the lunch, Jere posed that question to Mr. Uberroth. "Well, we do need a velodrome," he answered. I still recall John Thompson looking a bit puzzled and asking: "What is a velodrome?" It turned out that was the venue for all the cycling events. "How much would it cost to build a velodrome?" Jere Thompson inquired. "The estimates are about $4 million," Peter responded. Before the lunch ended, the velodrome idea became a reality. After the tremendously successful Olympics, Peter Uberroth was named Time Magazine's "Person of the Year". 7-Eleven came out of the tie-in with our own bicycle team. It competed successfully for several years on the national and international stage. The Olympics also ended up with a world class velodrome. I remember that we sponsored trips to the games for our top store people and franchisees. We housed everyone on cruise ships at Long Beach. Bob Hope came out and entertained the folks. The Olympic experience resonated within the company for a long time. Bill Scott, a marketing pro from the Stanford Agency, handled the Olympic advertising/PR duties for Southland. In big commitments, it is always good to have a specific person responsible for getting things done. Bill did a terrific job.

Sports relationships can be a good thing if everything adds up. "Sports" in general can be a great unifier, both for participants and spon-sors. Although I no longer serve in corporate PR, an idea for a sports tie-in has been floating around in my mind for a while. I will put it out there for anyone who might be looking for some-thing. I believe this idea could be a winner for the giants like Facebook, Google and Twitters of the tech galaxy and perhaps a Nike, Verizon or ATT of the corporate world. It consists of start-ing an umbrella organization called A SPORT FOR EVERYBODY. There are dozens, maybe hundreds, of different sports available for peo-ple to follow, take part in or support. The lead organization could farm out various sports for individual sponsorship. You could have a foot-ball, basketball and baseball sponsor for the big-time sports and other sponsors for the lesser-known sports. There might be promotional tie-ins for products like T-shirts, backpacks, coffee mugs, baseball caps and anything that could identify someone as backing a particular sport. You might consider organizing Zoom meetings for enthusiasts from around the world. Could somebody sign up for more than one sport? Absolutely! The spiritual purpose of such an umbrella sponsorship of A SPORT FOR EVERYBODY would be twofold: (1) Community and (2) Connection. These twin goals would hopefully result in creating "inclusivity". If we are to move forward in a contentious and frac-tured world, we need to find ways for people to get "included". I think human beings that feel included will be less stressed out, depressed and feeling abandoned and alone. Who knows? Maybe somewhere, a teenager that might be contemplating suicide could find community and connection with a group of fellow skateboarders, gamers, archers, volleyball, cricket, billiards, ping pong or whatever sports participants chose. Helping people to reach out and connect with others through a mutual interest in specific sports might possibly change the world for the better. It may be worth considering for a big idea thinker.

8

Spirituality, Religion And Finding Your Company's Purpose

You probably have many fine employees in your company who "belong" to a formal church or religious teaching. More than likely, they probably enjoy worshipping on a weekly (or more often) basis with a community of friends and like-minded believers. As an ordained minister, I say God bless anyone who makes a commitment to a church, synagogue, mosque or wherever a religious flock might choose to gather. Organized religion can and does do incredible and wonderful things. There is tremendous power in a committed church group. In the U. S., we are blessed with many excellent and varied churches, The U. S. religious community offers a plethora of belief systems to suit everyone. For many people, "church" is the center of their personal universe, along with family and work. I say more power to churchgoers. Yet, organized religion is not for everybody. In fact, a huge number of the 18-29 age group is opting out of standard religious practices. They bring their independent brand of worship to the altars of Instagram, TikTok, Twitter and dozens of other lesser- known internet platforms. There are also atheists and agnostics present in the non-religious world. What is going on? I believe religion and spirituality are two different things. I do think that God created each of us (believers and non-believers) with a divine spark at the core of our being. It represents our individual "God particle". The common denominator is "love". Almost anyone can sense a natural feeling of love rising when we see the beauty of nature, new-born babies, beloved pets, and a host of other wonderful things that inhabit our glorious planet. Would you ever turn away from a rainbow?

While religion is a choice, I think spirituality exists in everyone. I believe that all of us are spiritual beings having a human experience. We need an inner connection between people throughout the world. Billions of us are now rubbing elbows on an ever more crowded planet. Our spiritual nature is the common denominator that unites us. For people to live in some degree of harmony, we need to somehow identify with that God Spirit in each other. Countless wars over many centuries show what happens when we choose to ignore our human and divine links. Most of us react favorably when someone touches that common spiritual spark. Discovering our inherent spirituality is possible for anyone, regardless of gender, race, ethnic background, economic and social status, or cultural barriers. We are all God's children at the seat of our souls.

Perhaps the best of all worlds would be to enjoy membership in a common community that recognized the spirituality in others. Whatever our religious paths, our overall goal should be to pursue and forge a lifelong sense of unity and Oneness with God and each other. Peace for the entire world might then become a possibility.

So, what are the specific steps to begin finding your company's spiritual purpose? If this is something you want to pursue, here would be my recommendations on how to get started. Let me preface them by saying that you should follow your own guidance. You know your company and your people better than anyone. If you want to pursue my suggestions, they are 100% non-proprietary. Be sure to add your own thoughts to the mix. We will offer you more ideas at the end of this book.

1. **Go Slow**—In the beginning of the process to explore your spiritual purpose, tread lightly. Talk to the trusted people close to you, both in and out of your Company. Do not rush headlong into anything. At this point, you are doing research and due diligence. I would consider emphasizing the word "explore" with people when asking for input. Ask about community needs. Think about the most obvious areas such as health, children's illnesses, women's

issues, hunger, safety, housing, aging, child abuse, crime, and the general topic that should appeal to everyone: how to make life easier for one and all. These are not easy times for anybody. One great need is how to bring our diverse nation together under the one designation of "I am an American", while allowing individual communities to retain their uniqueness. Look for emerging issues. Who would have expected a global pandemic to upend the entire world?

2. **Brainstorm with your core group**—Be sure to include your PR and Community Relations people in the process. They probably understand the needs out there as well as anyone. Be sure that racial and ethnic communities are consulted and given leadership roles once a purpose or "cause" is identified. Don't forget to brainstorm with people you trust. Of course, you already know the rules of brainstorming. All ideas get honored. Nothing is dismissed out of hand. You want radical thinking. Pay special attention to what specific demographic, gender and age groups have to say. Be sure you note the differences and preferences between the young and old. Get people involved who understand the digital world.

3. **Pray and meditate.**—This might be a
dealbreaker for many corporate types.
The more "practical" folks might feel this
is too much of a "religious" or touchy-feely
step. It is not. Remember Jesus' famous
"Sermon on the Mount" when he told the
people "Ask and you shall receive. Seek
and you will find. Knock and the door will
be opened unto you." (Matthew 7:7) You
need to engage The Holy Spirit in this
important process. However, I would not
make a big deal about this aspect of exploring possibilities. For those folks un-
comfortable with "religion", explain this
is more of a "spiritual" step. But do not
let it become a contentious subject. If
someone wants to opt out of prayer and
meditation, allow them to take a pass.
Know that when you seek God's wisdom,
it will arrive in one form or other. If no
guidance comes back in the silence, the
answer may be communicated in a different way. God possesses many avenues of
getting our attention. Be patient. An-
swers will come. God always finds the
perfect moment to offer divine guidance.

4. **Break "Spiritual Purpose" gently to the
people who will carry out the program—**
By all means, get input and feedback
from the people on the frontlines of any
program you choose. Listen to their ad-

vice and concerns. Ask for their common-sense opinions. There is absolutely such a thing as "corporate wisdom". It involves the collective common-sense wisdom of everybody involved with the company. It represents a powerful corporate asset. Most organizations have a certain number of wise employees who are not high up on the organizational chart. Yet, their ideas and what they think could matter the most. I am sure you already know who they are.

5. **Get to know and build a relationship with the key people that run your charity or "cause".**—In fact, it would be good to meet these people before you make any commitment. Do not be afraid to ask for references. Visit their offices. This should not be a lengthy process. However, you may get an immediate vibe about the people with whom you would be interacting. If someone gets upset about transparency (they also may want a reference from you) then consider their reaction as a red flag.

6. **Explore websites and the social media presence of any group you might be considering.**—Understand there are some fruitcakes and bad actors out there. Do not be bashful about checking out anybody and everybody. Be wary of secretive and proprietary acting organizations.

They could be hiding something. People who engage in "mean Tweets" should be non-starters.

7. **Think hard before choosing a program identified with a specific denomination or religious group.**—I would never say never, but if you decide to go with any denomination, church or any other religious organization, you could be making somebody else mad. An exception might be donating to an Interfaith or Church Alliance Group that helps everyone. You want to build goodwill, not create problems.

8. **Seek a real partnership with your "cause".**—Do not be a passive participant in any relationship. Never be content with just writing a check once a year. Checks are nice, but you and your charitable partner will get much more out of a dynamic relationship. Hopefully, it will offer a sense of excitement and fulfillment for both parties. In addition, remember that your employees represent one of your most important publics. Bring them into the reasoning behind your spiritual purpose.

9. **If possible, do a test market before going company-wide.** —Sometimes it may not be possible to test market your "purpose".

For example, when 7-Eleven partnered with MDA and the Jerry Lewis Labor Day Telethon, we only had a few months to get everyone on board. Still, doing a test before rolling a program out company-wide offers some advantages. You may find out what not to do. Problems usually service sooner rather than later.

10. **Make yourself the person ultimately accountable for the project's success or failure.** —Of course, many other people in your company should be involved. But do not just introduce the idea and then fade out of sight. When something important involves your company, you should be there for the takeoff and the landing. One other thought: whatever spiritual purpose you finally select, search for the undeniable "Truth" that it contains. It should offer a "cause" so strong that it can withstand scrutiny from any angle.

9

Other Southland And 7-Eleven PR Projects: There Might Be An Idea Here For You

The Southland Corporation, its 7-Eleven Stores and our regional dairies had many worthwhile projects that allowed us to support our various communities. Here is a thumbnail description that might be helpful in finding your company's own spiritual purpose.

1. **THE MARCH OF DIMES**—At one time, Southland was the largest corporate sponsor of the March of Dimes and their campaign against birth defects. From re-searching them today, it appears MOD has begun focusing on "preemie" births, of which there are approximately 360,000 every year. This is an outstanding organi-zation that began with the terrible polio epidemic in the mid-1950s. I had the priv-ilege of introducing Dr. Jonas Salk in 1980 in Detroit as MOD was celebrating

the 25th anniversary of the Salk Vaccine. Surely the eradication of polio represents one of the greatest medical achievements of the last century. I would heartily recommend that any company consider the March of Dimes for a potential tie-in. MOD is involved with women's health issues, children and family issues.

2. **CHILDHELP USA**—The problem of child abuse never seems to go away. Childhelp USA has been around for more than 60 years. It was founded in 1959 by Sara O'Meara and Yvonne Fedderson, two young Hollywood actresses. These two amazing and hard-working women have never stopped in their efforts to help abused and neglected children. You will not meet a more dedicated and dynamic pair. They started Children's Village USA in Beaumont, California in 1976 as a place where abused children could go to reestablish their lives. In 1982, the Childhelp USA National Abuse Hotline was instituted. In 2000, Entertainer Merv Griffin gifted Childhelp with his 192-acre Wickenburg Inn and Dude Ranch preserve in Arizona. It is now named the Childhelp Merv Griffin Village of Arizona. Also that year, the United States House of Representatives unanimously passed a bill supporting "The Childhelp

National Day of Hope" that remembers
the children who have died from abuse
and neglect. I am not sure how active
Sara and Yvonne are in the day-to-day
operations of Childhelp, but they are incredible advocates for the welfare of children. You would do well to learn more
about them. Meet them if you can. They
are worthy of your support.

3.   **THE NATIONAL WILDLIFE FEDERA-
     TION**—Southland did its first ever na-
     tional PR program with the NWF. We
     first called on them at their Washington,
     D. C. area headquarters in 1974. To say
     they were skeptical of getting involved
     with any corporation, much less a conve-
     nience store chain from Texas, is an un-
     derstatement. They are correctly
     protective of their pristine reputation.
     When we met with Jim Davis, NWF's
     Creative Director, he warned us that any
     of relationship with a company like 7-
     Eleven was unlikely. We asked Jim one
     basic question: "What do you all need that
     is not in your budget" Jim did not hesi-
     tate. He said "The American bald eagle is
     endangered in the lower U. S. We need a
     refuge for the eagle within the contiguous
     48 states. We have scouted some loca-
     tions, but just do not have the money to
     proceed right now." We probed a little

further: "Exactly how much are we talking about?" Jim Davis responded that the NWF had found some property in South Dakota but the asking price was slightly above $250,000. Our PR group went back to Dallas and did some brainstorming. Somebody brought up an interesting question: "What else is endangered besides the bald eagle?" We called the NWF and they faxed us (yes, faxes were big in those days) a list of all species they considered endangered. It was an interesting array of creatures and included animals, birds and even insects. Dan McCurdy, one of the folks in our brainstorming group, had an idea that we could create interest for other endangered species besides the bald eagle. He suggested commissioning artwork from the NWF and then putting the designs on special Slurpee cups. The cups could even become a collector's item. We proposed that 7-Eleven donate a penny from every cup sold. Since the company would be selling approximately four million Slurpees in June, July and August, that meant the campaign might bring in $400,000. That was more than enough for the Eagle refuge. Now THAT is a big idea. We also needed a campaign theme to tie everything together. Don Coburn, a creative wunderkind in the Stanford Agency, came up with a brilliant line: "SAVE A LIVING THING". You might have heard of "D. L. Coburn". He won the Pulitzer Prize for Drama in 1978 for his iconic play "The Gin Game" starring Hume Cronyn and Jessica Tandy. At any rate, we took the idea back to Jim Davis and the NWF. They loved it. At the end of the campaign, we presented the NWF with a check for the eagle refuge, with money left over. A couple of years later, The Karl Mundt (named for the long-time South Dakota senator) National Refuge for the American Bald Eagle became a reality. It was a win-win for everybody. There might even be somebody in your company that collected a set of those Slurpee Endangered Species cups. Nearly 50 years later, they are still available on ebay and other places.

4. **U. S. MARINES/TOYS FOR TOTS PROGRAM**—This was a wonderful tie-in program for our 7 Eleven Stores. We were natural partners as a drop off site for the Christmas toys. I cannot say enough good things about the Marines' involvement in providing toys to children in need. Since 1947, the U. S. Marine Corps has distributed 604 million toys to 272 million children. Toys For Tots already has some high profile corporate sponsors such as

FedEx, UPS, Target and Disney. They are also clear on the financial commitment they expect. The tab is $100,000 for a corporate "sponsor" and $25,000 to be listed as a corporate donor. This program can generate local excitement. Many TV stations do local news remotes from the drop off sites. I recall an event near the Chicago River and Michigan Avenue at high noon in the mid 70's. Mayor Daley had declared a "Toys for Tots" day, Olivia Newton-John was there to lend support (she was very big then) and the U. S. Marine Band performed. Martin Janis, our terrific Chicago PR guy, turned out tons of local media. It was a great day for everyone involved.

5. **RUNAWAY HOTLINE**—I have not heard much about this excellent idea lately, but Southland partnered with the governor's office in the state of Texas to offer a special hotline for runaway kids to reconnect with their parents. We called it "Operation Peace of Mind". I am sure this kind of service is or could be offered now by a myriad of digital platforms. Connecting runaway kids with their worried families is still a good idea. Getting reconnected has become an issue for every family in crisis today. Anything positive that can

be done to to address this serious problem would help.

6. **TEACHER OF THE YEAR**—For many years, our Oak Farms Dairies in Texas did a "Teacher of the Year" recognition program for state educators. The winning teacher got a cash prize, a sizeable donation to his/her school and much deserved recognition. In October, 1985, our keynote speaker at the Dallas event was Christa McAuliffe. It was such a privilege to meet and talk with her. The Challenger was scheduled to lift off in early 1986 and Christa was so excited to tell everyone about it. She was a wonderful teacher and person. This national hero left behind an outstanding legacy for us all.

7. **LOCAL/REGIONAL/NATIONAL SPORTS TIE-INS**—Southland, 7-Eleven and our dairies all participated in many sports sponsorships over the years. Of course, the 1984 Olympics spawned our 7-Eleven cycling team for a while. Our fledgling Chief Auto Parts Stores even dabbled with NASCAR one season. That can be extremely expensive and did not last, but at least I was able to experience the Daytona 500 in 1984. Without a doubt, it is one of the most exciting events in all sports. Whether you are a race car fan or not, NASCAR personifies excite-

ment. College sports sponsorships are huge now. That is a good area to explore for local tie-ins, especially in sports other than football or basketball. Getting more involved with a local college can lead to positive things like scholarships. Helping people obtain an education is always a good thing. I do not know which sponsors are big now with Little League and Pop Warner ball now, but sports involving kids should always be considered. Many of these types of sponsorships flourish with local businesses. My first Little League uniform was furnished by the local Coca-Cola bottler. Many folks love golf and tennis. As far as the major tournaments are involved, you are talking big bucks. Unless you are a multi-billion-dollar corporation, those are probably out of reach. But companies like the Travelers, Wells Fargo Bank and the Valero Energy Company do outstanding jobs with their big-time PGA events. They have raised many millions for good causes. The main consideration in any sports tie-in is budget When big-time sports, professional athletes, ego and emotions get tangled up, common sense can go out the window. Try to keep everything on a practical level. There is such a thing as spending too much of the company's money. It is called diminishing returns. Avoid them.

8. **CHILDREN'S MIRACLE NETWORK HOSPITALS**—After retiring from Southland and prior to beginning my ministerial studies at Unity Village, I worked for a year in my hometown of Temple, TX for the McLane Company. Drayton McLane, Jr. is son of the founder and one of the most outstanding businesspeople in the entire country. The original McLane distribution network was first sold to Drayton's long-time tennis partner Sam Walton, the founder of Wal-Mart. It is now owned by Warren Buffet. The McLane Company itself is still working in a myriad of other successful endeavors. Drayton McLane Jr. is the epitome of an involved corporate leader. He has been involved with the Children's Miracle Network Hospitals for decades. CMNH is an excellent and well-run charity that raises funds for children's hospitals in the U. S. It was founded by Marie Osmond, actor John Schneider and several others in 1983. CMNH has raised more than $7 billion for 158 hospitals. Corporate sponsors include many national and international names. Walmart alone has raised more than $1 billion. Other corporate sponsors include Sam's Club, Costco, Dairy Queen, Delta Airlines, and many well-known fraternities and sororities. I would recommend that you check out

CMNH if you are interested in getting involved with the health of children.

9. **UNITED WAY**—For many companies, the United Way remains the charitable gold standard. The Southland Corporation and its subsidiaries have contributed tens of millions of dollars over the years to United Way. I do not see how anyone could go wrong considering them for a tie-in. Many of you are probably working with UW already.

10

Allowing Meditation To Awaken Your Creativity And Spirituality

Let's talk more about meditation. It is finally receiving its due as a healing practice. Meditating has been medically proven to lower blood pressure, reduce stress, and even improve your heart health. Many medical professionals recommend it without reservation. If you are thinking about starting your own personal meditation practice, I want to offer you a 5-step process that might help you get started. When beginning to meditate, please do not put any expectations on yourself. There is no wrong way to meditate. Your time in the silence belongs only to you—and God. Once you begin experiencing the serenity of the silence, you will want to go there often. Meditation can also enhance your creativity. Many divine ideas that changed history probably began during somebody's time alone with God and the universe. There is great power in the silence. Meditation often brings forth insightful and creative thinking. It is hard to hatch great ideas if you never stop and listen to your inner wisdom.

THE FIVE STEP MEDITATION PROCESS:

1. **RELAXATION**—Find a quiet place where you will not be disturbed. Sit with both feet on the floor. Put your hands in your lap, palms upward. Now inhale five deep breaths, one at a time, through your nose. Release each one slowly, breathing through your open mouth. Quiet your body and mind by relaxing totally into the silence.

2. **CONCENTRATION**—Center your thoughts on the spiritual energy within you. Feel God's presence in and around you.

3. **MEDITATION**—In quiet reflection, experience the power of your own divinity. Keep your mind focused on the silence. Try to keep your brain quiet and clutter free. Stay in the now moment Let the world turn without your presence.

4. **REALIZATION**—This is where the magic happens. It is all about melding into Oneness with God. Realizing God's Presence within you causes everything to fall into place. A sense of peace prevails as you align yourself with God. You may even discern a still, small voice. Spirit may not make Itself known to you yet. Do not give up on your meditation efforts. Keep ex-

ploring the silence. Be patient and expectant. Any time meditating is a beneficial expenditure of your time. Nothing exceeds the realization of becoming as One with your inner spirit.

5. **APPRECIATION**—Be grateful for any time you spend alone in the silence with God. You are establishing intimate communication with your Creator. Give thanks for this time to explore a divine relationship with your Higher Power.

Remember, less formal and briefer meditations also count. There are no lost moments in the silence. In a short while, people will start to see a difference in you. Your peacefulness and serenity will become evident to everyone.

11

The Future May Hold The Key To Your Company's Spiritual Purpose

The world is changing—fast. If you cannot identify your spiritual purpose, maybe it is not ready
for you quite yet. Let me offer some ideas about
what may be coming down the road (or is
already here). In my opinion, these areas of
present and coming developments may offer
your company something to consider in finding
your spiritual purpose.

INFORMATION—We live in an information
age. In fact, there is almost too much knowledge—except when you need it. Delivering relevant information fast can make someone's time
more productive. How can your company be of
service in terms of providing useful information
in a timely manner? For brainstorming sake,
let's imagine you are in the food business or
even a retail supermarket chain. Of course, you
have the Thursday food section in the paper and
online. What if you found out specifically what
food or dish someone likes—and then triggered

a text or e-mail anytime news came up about that dish or product. You do not have to wait for the weekend. Most people are chowing down on something 24/7. OK, why is that a spiritual purpose? They might even use that extra time you saved them to perform a good deed for someone. Providing human beings anything that simplifies their life can reduce stress. Parenting is another area that can use focused information. Find out what information parents need with their child-raising duties and help them get it. Concerned parents always appreciate having extra knowledge when it comes to their children. There is a constant flow of information streaming forth from endless sources. Yet, what percentage is truly relevant? What about the latest Internet scams? If your company has access to this type of information, you could be doing somebody a real service besides saving them money. "Alerts" of any kind can be valuable. Everybody knows about weather alerts. At any given time, people are sitting in an office somewhere (like at the doctor or dentist). What are they doing while they wait? Of course, they are checking their cell phones. What about a service that provides up to date traffic alerts from where you might be at any given moment? That might even already exist. Maybe a news alert could be updated every half hour: "HERE'S WHAT HAPPENED IN THE LAST 30 MINUTES". How about a new App: "THE LAST 30 MINUTES" that could grab some attention? Do some of these ideas seem far out to you? Think about them the next time you check your cell

phone in line at the supermarket or sitting in a
waiting room

HEALTH—The covid-19 pandemic has been the
most dramatic health development of the century so far. It has triggered considerable interest in health-related issues. I believe this
represents only the beginning of how "health"
issues will dominate our lives in the years
ahead. We all want to know more about how we
can live healthier. The pandemic has affected
the physical and emotional health of everyone.
Stress is through the roof. Suicides have spiked.
Drug use is soaring. Depression has impacted
many people. We are having a once-in-a-lifetime
crisis sorting out our mental health problems. I
believe many serious "health" concerns are just
beginning to surface. A corporation looking for a
"cause" or spiritual purpose would do well to
explore "health". Helping anyone achieve a
healthier life is a win-win for everyone.

INCLUSIVITY—Society has been fragmenting
for many years. The "tribal" aspect of community has become apparent. Yet, the real
strength of our nation has always been in our
"unity". Anything that promotes togetherness
rather than highlighting our differences has
long term potential. I love it when someone now
living here from another country or culture
exhibits pride in being a part of America. I
remember thinking a few times: "That person is
much more American than me." I believe any
company that promotes inclusivity is on the
right track. In a related area, more people are

isolated and living alone. Adding to that poten-
tially negative trend is that (at least until the
pandemic) human beings are living longer.
Being alone for any length of time can threaten
someone's health. Being by yourself when you
are turning 90 or 100 is both painful and dangerous. I believe we need each other. "Not leaving anyone behind" can apply to more than just
the battlefield. Human connections should be
available for anyone who feels isolated. Online
Zoom meetings during the pandemic demon-
strated how technology can help maintain connections. Human beings need to know that
somebody cares. Brainstorming how your company could bring people together via Zoom and
other methods is an endeavor worthy of who you
are. Perhaps a collection of "Neighborhood
Zooms" could bring a mixture of races, genders
and ages together to exchange ideas. We are all
so much more alike than different. We just need
to know one another better.

ISSUES AFFECTING THE ELDERLY—I still
recall watching a news story on TV a few years
ago. The news anchor reported that a certain
"elderly" person had been injured in a car acci-
dent. He then stated the man's age. I felt a bit
shocked when I learned the victim was 10 years
younger than me. It is never easy being identified in a new demographic. I am here to remind
everyone that the older people among us are
coping with a technologically complicated, confusing and speeded-up world. Close family connections are sometimes non-existent. Older
folks who live alone worry about lying on the

floor after a fall. They could be there for hours or even days. It is not a pleasant thought. On top of normal worries, the effect of the covid-19 pandemic on the elderly will reverberate for many years. So many have died alone and apart from loved ones. But "ageism" itself is a real but underreported problem. I believe anything a company can do to help older Americans cope with life will be noticed and appreciated. Most everybody is someone's mom, dad, son or daughter. This area blends nicely with "Health Issues" in general. One of the most vexing problems we face now is Alzheimer's Disease. The Baby Boomers are about to enter that phase of their lives. Unless we find cures or treatments, our society faces a grim new reality that affects practically everyone. Perhaps your company could do something to help in this area.

BULLYING—In 2008, my wife Jan Carmen Liles watched an Oprah Winfrey show about kids being bullied. It inspired her to write a book about the problem entitled BECAUSE YOU MATTER. After the book was printed, Jan and I traveled around the Twin Cities doing book readings for first through fourth graders. We asked the kids "Have you ever been bullied?" At every session, about 90% raised their hands. We are talking about children 6-10 who have already experienced bullying. Many said the bullies were older children in their own families. Bullying can decimate self-esteem, even for the strongest kid. There is much more that needs addressing in this important area. Being bullied can result in negative consequences.

Some things are being done, but much more is needed. Let's do everything we can to save the children.

CONVENIENCE—Making something more convenient always garners positive attention. 7-Eleven invented an entire industry by making shopping convenient and available 24/7. Amazon became one of the most successful companies in world history, just by delivering everything you want from its door to yours. How can your services and products be made more convenient to customers? Although this may seem more like a sales promotional tool than spiritual purpose, it could be both. Making human life easier can be stress reducing. It might be something to brainstorm. Look for the Big Idea that can change the world.

EMPLOYEES AND FRANCHISEES—Besides your customers, your employees (and franchisees) represent your most important asset. What do they need to enrich their lives? How can your relationship be improved with those who serve your customers? Besides money, what can you do to make their lives better? The pandemic has caused many shifts in relationships. How can you recalibrate the bond between you and employees? A "Franchisee Appreciation Day" or "Employee Appreciation Day" perhaps?

MAKING LIFE FUN AGAIN—Joy could be one of the hardest things to retrieve in a world beset with division and mistrust. Rekindling happiness for others is a definite spiritual act, worthy of thought and pursuit. This might be another topic for a brainstorming session. Make nothing off limits as you consider ways to reintroduce fun back into daily living. When was the last time you laughed at something? Personally, I have had enough grimness to last a lifetime. There are so many people, from every category of life, that need their spirits boosted. Be a light for them. Let us bring back fun and a reason to smile.

A Word About Politics

I come from a political family. Both my father (Winston L. Liles) and grandfather (A. L. Liles) served on the Temple, TX city council. My mother (Edith Liles) was a member of the Texas State Democratic Executive Committee in 1948. That was the year a young Texas Congressman named Lyndon Baines Johnson won an 87-vote "landslide" victory that made him a U. S. Senator. There was much talk that year about voting irregularities. The Democratic Executive Committee, of which my mother was a member, had to certify the election. The vote was 17-16 in LBJ's favor, with my mother voting for him. In addition, when President Harry S Truman stopped at the M-K-T terminal in Temple during his whistle-stop tour in the 1948 presidential campaign, my mother and father were two of about 30 people escorted onto the train to shake hands with President Truman, his wife Bess and daughter Margaret. Besides all of that, my amazing sister (Linda Liles) was the State Youth Campaign manager for Texas Governor Price Daniel in the mid-1950s when she was a teenager. I also recall Gov. Daniel taking my dad aside privately at a campaign rally and asking his opinion about the upcoming election. I give you this information to preface my opinion about mixing your company's spiritual purpose with politics. I would try to avoid confusing them. A spiritual purpose should ideally benefit everyone, regardless of political affiliation. I understand that many companies feel they must participate in the political process. In my opinion, politics and spirituality are opposites. Politics and politicians are constantly changing. Spiritual Truths are eternal and unchanging. Despite what some churches (both Democrat and Republican) may tell you, I am absolutely certain that God is 100% apolitical.

12

Corporate Culture: What Is It?

Whether you know it or not, your company has a "culture". It consists of everyone who has ever been associated with your organization and everything that has occurred in its history. If your corporation or business has been around for a while, the culture has millions of impressions floating around in the ethers. When you try to change or deviate from your culture, problems can surface. It is akin to revising the Harry Potter books and making them about an elderly couple in a Florida retirement center. When you try to change a long-held culture, strange things can happen. The change could be positive and productive. Other times, it can backfire and jeopardize the company. Finding your company's spiritual purpose should be a positive add-on to a "good" culture or a definite help in reversing a current culture problem.

I had the privilege of writing the history of The Southland Corporation, founded in Dallas, TX in 1927 to sell block ice. The invention of the refrigerator changed the course of its history, but by that time Southland were also selling other items. The creation of the convenience store industry followed. Now, there are more than 150,000 c-stores in the U. S. alone.

In Southland and 7-Eleven's case, the culture was primarily created by founder Joe C. (Jodie) Thompson, Jr. In interviewing long-time employees for the company history book, this is the most prevalent comment I heard about Mr. Thompson: "He was the greatest person I ever met." The second generation of Thompsons: John (who passed in 2005), Jere and Jodie III were all great people. Let me share a couple of stories about what "culture" meant to them.

In 1975, one of our Stanford Agency in-house copywriters died at a relatively young age. Bob Peck was a former musician who played in the Tex Beneke Orchestra back in the 1940s and 50s. Bob had dated the band's girl singer (Eydie Gorme) before she married Steve Lawrence. Bob found his lovely and long-time wife Mary and they settled down in Dallas. He landed a job as a writer for Southland's ad department. It was led by the great Bob Stanford, a bona fide creative genius. The two Bobs loved each other. Peck had the quickest wit and most infectious laugh of probably anyone I ever met. He coined the name "BIG GULP". You may have enjoyed one or two of them. At any rate, Bob Peck's unexpected death shocked everyone. I was not present when this scene unfolded at the Peck's house after the funeral. The Thompson brothers were there to extend their sympathy to Mary Peck for the loss of her beloved husband. The Peck family had five children and several of them were still living at home. What I heard was that Mary was taken aside by the Thompsons and gifted with a multi-year lease on a 7-Eleven store. She was literally given her own store. I do not know how much money was involved, or even if the story was entirely true. I never asked, because it was so Thompson-like, there was no reason to question it.

Another incident I did see up close and personal. At our second Labor Day Telethon in 1977 in Las Vegas, 7-Eleven and McDonalds were running neck and neck to be the #1 corporate sponsor. McDonald's made their final presentation right before 7-Eleven's last slot. The Big Mac people announced $3.5 million, a larger number than what 7-Eleven had done during our first year as a corporate sponsor in 1976. I was backstage with John and Jere Thompson prior to them going onstage with Jerry Lewis. John Thompson turned to me and asked, "How much are we going to announce?" I told him that our donation would be $3.2 million, about what we had done in the first year. John did not hesitate. He turned to his brother Jere and said "I'm going to add $400.000 to our total. If the money does not come in by the time the stores stop counting, you and I can make it up with a personal donation. Is that OK with you?" Jere did not hesitate. "Absolutely", he said. The two Thompson brothers shook hands. They walked on, greeted Jerry and announced 7-Eleven had raised $3.6 million. We remained the #1 corporate sponsor.

Their father was a fanatic about wanting to reward Southland's employees, especially the people on the front line. He was one of the first CEOs to make "Profit Sharing" part of Southland's corporate culture. I can't tell you how many store people retired with six-figure (or more) pensions. Most of the Plan's assets then were in the form of store or building leases and company stock. The gains every year were almost always double digits. One of the highlights every year was receiving your annual "Profit Sharing Statement". There were many whoops heard up and down the halls of our offices. Again, that is building a corporate culture whose worth is impossible to measure.

What about your company culture? I trust it is good. It represents a prize possession that will pay outstanding dividends through the years. If your culture is lacking in something, I submit it is never too late to change things. Finding your spiritual purpose is an excellent beginning.

13

So, What If Your Choice For A Spiritual Purpose Says "Thanks, But No Thanks"?

You have done your brainstorming, practiced some deep meditation, asked for divine guidance and settled on a solid choice for your company's spiritual purpose. Then, you take the idea to your selection and they surprise you by saying "no". Whatever the reason, that can be hard to hear. Having to go back and report that your company's overture was rejected can seem embarrassing. Believe me, it is not. Here is why. One thing that I have learned over the years about the Spiritual Path concerns something called "Divine Order". If a relationship is meant to happen in God's universe, nothing can stop it. Everything falls smoothly in place. Possible obstacles fade away. Momentum and progress occur naturally. Nothing seems like a stretch and strain. On the other hand, if even small things erupt into big problems, that is a definite wake-up call to rethink your strategy. If things do not pan out with one idea, do not see it as a reflection on you or your company. Sometimes,

even with the best of ideas, the timing may not
be right for one or both parties. Try to view any
misfire as a sign that God has something better
in mind. By the way, this attitude can also work
well in your personal life. Remember that old
Garth Brooks song from a few years ago: "I
thank God for unanswered prayers". There is
much truth to that sentiment. There is always
more than one path to reach your destination.
Keep telling yourself: "If not this, then something better." Trust God to keep that promise.

Let me tell you a time recently when one of my
ideas was rejected. After my wife Jan passed in
2017, I moved back home to my native Texas. I
filled a few pulpits by doing Sunday talks at
Unity churches in Temple and Austin. But my
active PR/Spiritual brain was also still function-
ing. It still conjured up a marketing idea every
now and then. In 2018, I received what seemed
a divine idea during one of my meditations. I
really liked the PBS news program "FRONT-
LINE". I thought then and still believe it offers
first-rate reporting and terrific insights. My
idea was for FRONTLINE to extend its brand
by starting a new program called
FRONTLINE/HEALTH. I believe that "health"
will be one of the most newsworthy topics this
century. I viewed FRONTLINE as the news program to become the "go-to" source on health
issues. I did some research and located the PBS
station in Boston that originates the program. I
did more online sleuthing and came up with a
specific name in their development department.
I took a chance and called her direct. After a

couple of minutes, I was somehow able to get the person on the line. I quickly explained that I was a former VP/PR for 7-Eleven and I had an idea for FRONTLINE. Her first question, before I could explain the idea, was "How did you get my name and number?" She did have the good graces to listen to my spiel. I explained the premise for the FRONTLINE/HEALTH spinoff. I even shared that I knew someone here in Texas who might consider underwriting part of the project. As I say, she was gracious enough to hear me out. But I could tell what she was thinking: "How did this guy with a Texas twang manage to come up with my number." She brushed me off politely and that was that. After the covid-19 pandemic hit the world in 2020, I thought about that conversation. Had FRONT-LINE acted on this divine idea in 2018 that had originated from an unusual source, who knows where things might have gone. As it turned out, FRONTLINE did eventually produce an outstanding broadcast on the pandemic. I do believe the health angle is still a good idea for some news organization There are still many pressing health care issues coming this way. Maybe a TV network or another PBS affiliate might decide to claim it. In this case, the timing (or maybe my Texas accent) just was not right. I absolutely do not take it personally. I am glad I made the call. If not this, something better.

Anybody can be off when it comes to evaluating opportunities. I recall one day in the early 1980s when Eric Norrington, one of our premier Southland PR pros, stepped into my office. He had just gotten off the telephone with the personal agent for a new female singer. Eric told me that the singer had asked the agent to specifically call 7-Eleven about sponsoring her first ever tour. "She sounds kind of interesting and they only want $5000 for a 10-city tour. However, there is one strange thing: she only has one name and it's sort of bizarre." "What is it?" I asked. "Madonna," Eric replied. My reaction was swift: "That's crazy," I almost shouted, "Absolutely not. We cannot afford to upset our Catholic customers. Tell them no." Chalk one up for me.

Let me share one more personal story about being rejected. Southland had done some business over the years with the Richards Group in Dallas. Stan Richards founded his award-winning agency many years ago. Over the years, it has been fabulously successful. You might remember the famous Tom Bodet commercials for Motel Six: "We'll leave the lights on for you." The Richards Group created that campaign and many more. Right before I retired from Southland, Stan interviewed me for a job with his agency. For whatever reason, he passed on hiring me. I am so grateful to him for making that decision. He did me an tremendous favor that I can never repay. Without question, I would have said "yes" had Stan offered me a job. Who would not want to work for the best ad agency in town? But because he said "No", I was able to move forward to my own spiritual path that led to the ministry.. If somebody says "no" to your company as a charitable partner, some day you may have the occasion to thank them as well. Thank you again, Stan.

On a personal note, there is one other "idea" floating around with right me now. It has not yet been fully revealed. It concerns my current residence in Temple, Texas. I was born and raised in Temple and graduated from high school here. It is a great and growing medium size city of 75,000 in central Texas off I-35, between Dallas and Austin. I was gone for many years, including 28 years in Dallas working in the corporate world and 17 years of ministry in Minnesota with my lovely wife Jan. I also spent nearly 10 years in the Kansas City area while associated with the Unity Movement and two years living near Michigan Avenue in Chicago after I retired from Southland. Yet, I have twice now returned to my hometown of Temple. I came back in 1989 to work for the McLane Company as their communications manager. I came back again nearly 30 years later after Jan made her transition in 2017. For some reason, I find myself drawn back here. I have no living relatives in Temple and only a handful of acquaintances and high school classmates. Yet, I keep coming back home. In my meditations, I have considered the religious definition of "temple". According to the dictionary, a "temple" is a religious building that is meant for "worshipping or praying". Of course, most temples tend to be associated with non-Christian religions like Islam, Judaism and Buddhism. Some sects of orthodox Christianity worship in temples as well. The word comes from the Latin *"templum"* which means "consecrated piece of ground" or "building for worship of a god." My hometown was founded on June 29, 1881 by Bernard Moore Temple, a railroad executive. My grandfather A. L. Liles was born in the area in 1880 before it became a city. My dad, Winston Liles, was a longtime employee of the Atchison, Topeka and Santa Fe Railroad's hub in Temple. Both the Santa Fe and Katy (MKT) Railroad have always been big here. There are also several major medical facilities located in Temple: Baylor Scott & White and the VA's Central Texas Medical System. The outstanding HEB grocery chain and Wal-Mart have distribution centers here. Temple has been a long-time home to Drayton McLane, Jr and the McLane Company.

At any rate, perhaps "temple" is my place to continue serving God after Jan's passing and my subsequent retirement from pulpit ministry. I have been writing spiritually oriented books since arriving back home in 2017. However, I also wonder if my Texas hometown might someday play a small role in a kind of spiritual renaissance. I believe the world might be ready for a new direction. In my opinion, we have been headed down a slippery slope for some time now. Anyway, I am open to seeing what being "in temple" might mean for me during my time remaining on the spiritual path (and on the planet). I have experienced many surprises so far along the way. Perhaps God still has one or two more trick shots in His golf bag. I plan to stay open and receptive to Her divine Will for My life. And I will probably do it "in Temple".

To that end, I have begun writing a series entitled "Classic Bible Chapters" that takes one individual Bible Chapter (from both the Old and New Testaments) and focuses on the messages the Biblical writers were trying to convey. The first three books in the series are: JOHN 14/The most Important Chapter in the New Testament; EPHESIANS 6/Putting on the Whole Armor of God; and EXODUS 20/The Ten Commandments. The Classic Chapter books are short and can be read in about an hour. My goal is to encourage more reading of God's Holy Word. There is so much comfort, guidance and encouragement available in these sacred pages. I think God created the Bible to help us navigate this thing called human life. Besides all of that, it has some fantastic stories that have great wisdom for today.

14

God Is Good — All The Time

I was raised in a Southern Baptist Church here in Temple. My sweet and long since departed mother was a Sunday School superintendent at the old Memorial Baptist Church on South 13th Street. Our pastor, while I was growing up, was Brother George Brown. If you did not feel the flames of hell lapping at your feet during one of his fire and brimstone harangues, you were not paying attention. I personally never saw anyone doze off during any of Brother Brown's powerful messages. Virtually no one sat in the front pew unless you wanted your britches scorched. When the last altar call ended, I was often happy to escape with my life.

I attended Baylor University in Waco after high school, 35 miles north up I-35. You may remember the Baylor Bears men's basketball team beating Gonzaga to win the NCAA championship in 2021. Baylor is a wonderful school and the largest Baptist college anywhere. There were no co-ed dorms during my time on campus.. Until the 1940s, men walked on one side of the street and women on the other. If anyone got caught smoking on the campus while I was in school, I never heard about it. I served as editor of The Baylor Lariat, the university's daily newspaper, during my senior year. I was once summoned to the President Billy White's office, along with my journalism professor, for advocating girl cheerleaders and dancing on the Baylor campus. They have had female cheerleaders for many years now, but I am still not sure about the dancing. I wrote no more wayward editorials after my chewing out by Dr. White. I think he even put my j-school professor on notice.

I was not anti-religious either in or after college. I was mainly focused on my corporate career at Southland and being a husband and dad. Our family did attend the First Methodist Church in Richardson, TX for a while. Leighton Farrell was the senior minister and he went on to bigger and better things. In the early 1980s, I was drawn to a large Baptist church, located in far north Dallas. The pastor was an outstanding young preacher who was also obviously going places. A famous Dallas woman who built a billion-dollar cosmetics empire believed in this dynamic minister as well. So, she gave him the money to build one of the first megachurches. At its height, thousands of religious seekers filled the pews every Sunday. I was one of them. Then, something went very wrong. Despite his success, the pastor was suddenly asked to leave. It turned out that an angry husband had showed up at the church one day complaining about the counseling techniques the pastor was using on his young wife. Before the scandal ran its course, there were about 20 other women receiving the same "counseling" at a nearby church-owned condo. The incident also taught me a valuable lesson. There really is a "devil" out there. The red-horned one is deadly smart in a cunning and baffling way. Whatever your human weaknesses, he already knows about them. You can expect probes and outright spiritual attacks when you least expect it. These thrusts usually surface just when everything is going along for you in a positive way. Everyone needs to stay alert. Your life can depend on it.

In the summer of 1985, my spiritual quest accelerated. I discovered meditation. I also found some old cassette tapes by a true American mystic named Joel Goldsmith. He founded the Infinite Way, a spiritual movement that employs meditation and focuses on our innate oneness with God. Although Joel passed in 1964, his talks and books ("THE ART OF MEDITATION") are still widely available. They are all over the You Tube Premium Channel. If you have never heard one of Joel's "classes", I would recommend you consider checking them out. It will introduce you to mystical thinking. So, during the fall of 1986, I was progressing with my spiritual exploration and practicing meditation. I began discerning the "still, small voice", which mystics say is connected to our "soul". It is the "Holy Spirit" that lives within us all. What I heard during my meditations was startling, unexpected and a bit disturbing. Without question, I

was being directed to leave my corporate PR job.
I was hearing that my two wonderful decades
with the best company headquartered in Dallas
would be ending soon. On the surface, everything still looked fine. During my 20 years with
Southland, we never experienced a single quarter when the profits did not exceed that of the
same quarter in the prior year. My inner guidance to leave the corporate world persisted
throughout October and November. I explored
my options. Southland had an early retirement
plan that, if your age and years of service
equaled 70, you could retire with some benefits
intact. After more prayer and meditation, I
made the scary decision to take the plunge. I
decided to follow God's direction and leave the
security of my career. I called Helen Osborne,
Jere W. Thompson's longtime secretary, to
schedule an appointment. She asked what the
meeting was about. I just mumbled something
about "a personal matter". When I sat down
with Jere in his office the next afternoon, I
explained that I was not unhappy but that it
might be time for me to go. Several months
before, Southland had invited an internationally
famous consulting firm to evaluate our current
direction. At least one of the consultants doing
the Southland study was involved some years
later in the Enron stock scandal. Anyway, these
guys all came across as the smartest guys in the
room. Somebody even wrote a book about the
firm with that exact title. These renowned consultants came back with the standard recom-
mendation: downsize. Cutting people is always

their first option. To my knowledge, Southland had never laid off anybody in its entire history. We were too busy growing and making money. When the first staff reductions came during the Spring of 1986, we lost five of the 35 people in our PR department. Of course, the cuts fell upon the employees with the longest careers. It was a definite shock to the company's paternalistic culture. It was as though a beloved grandpa had hauled off and slapped somebody during Thanksgiving dinner. There was shock, disbelief, and anger. If our great company was losing money or going downhill, it might have been understandable. But the reverse was true. I believe these consultant-driven layoffs did more to reverse our positive 60-year culture than anything in the company's history. The damage was immediate. The acclaimed consulting group then left town and moved on to their next "victim", I mean "project". In their wake, it left behind a model company that was now questioning itself.

I did not cite the effect of the consultant's recommendations to Jere Thompson as a reason for my decision to retire. I took full responsibility of wanting to opt out early. Nor did I mention the spiritual direction that I was receiving in meditation. I just kept repeating the same mantra: "I think it is time for me to go." He looked at me and I recall him saying: "Are you absolutely sure about your decision? There are not many jobs like yours in the classifieds."

Of course, Jere was spot on. Yes, corporate sala-ries have exploded over the past 35 years. But I was still making a base salary of $100,000 with a $50,000 bonus if we met our profit goals (which we always did). My job was not only well-paying, I found it fulfilling. We were given the opportunity to do wonderful things. Then, I did something that was totally unscripted. I did not even consider this possibility before sitting down in Jere's office. Out of nowhere, I blurted out, "Yes, I know I will not be able to replace my income. What I would like is a salary continua-tion for two years." I probably had the same sur-prised on my face that Jere showed on his. He sat back, gave me a serious look and said: "Well, I can't make a decision like that by myself. I will need to talk to John first. After I visit with him about it, I will get back to you." Then, I did something else that was uncharacteristic of me. As we stood to say good-bye, instead of shaking hands, I gave Jere a big hug. It was the second time for him to look surprised. But, to his credit, he hugged me back. Two corporate execs embracing each other in the middle of the day! You must be kidding. Later that afternoon, Jere called me. "John and I talked it over," he told me, "We can't give the $50K bonus because you won't be here. But John agreed we could con-tinue your $100,000 base salary for the next two years. You have done a great job for Southland. We both think you deserve it." I stammered out my gratitude and appreciation. I know now it was God's way of saying "If you will follow My divine guidance, I promise to pick up the tab."

Another conclusion: if something is meant to happen, the doors will swing open so that you can walk through them with ease."

Something else happened after the meeting with Jere and before my end of the year departure date. Jean Muller, Southland's assistant PR director, offered to arrange a meeting for me with Albert Gaulden. Jean explained that Albert was founder and head of the Sedona Intensive, a spiritual think tank in Arizona. A few years later, a popular best seller entitled *THE CELESTINE PROPHECY* would be dedicated to Albert by the book's author James Redfield. Albert swung by Dallas once a year to meet with his clients in the area, of which Jean was one. I agreed to the meeting without any expectations. I can honestly say that the one hour and fifteen minutes I spent with Albert Gaulden changed my life forever. Just the day before the session, I had received a tentative job offer from an international company with a large presence in Dallas. I would be heading up their local PR operation. The money was fabulous, one and a half times what I was making at Southland. I had scheduled an appointment with the company the following week to discuss the offer. The Richards Group possibility had fallen through, so I would be free to consider staying in corporate PR. As I sat down with Albert, he surprised me by saying "I hear you are thinking about taking another PR job." He was not a mind reader. I had already confided to Jean that I had been approached. Then, he said, "Allen, you have the free will choice to say yes. However, I wanted to share a different perspective with you. So far in your life, you have spent your time making other people and companies look good. That is fine. But I want to suggest that you might take the time now to do something important for yourself." What's that?" I asked. "Why don't you consider finding out who you really are." That thought had never crossed my mind. Albert continued: "God is giving you the time and the money to do that," he said, "Instead of rushing into another corporate job, take the opportunity to discover what is really important to you." Then, he added something else. "I get a strong vibration from you about Russia. I see you writing either books or columns about your experiences in Russia. Are you planning a trip there?" That was not something I had considered. But, let me tell you what happened in 1995, nearly 10 years later. I happened to be watching coverage of President Bill Clinton visiting Boris Yeltsin in Moscow. There was a group shot at a dinner given for Clinton by the Russian leader. There, attending the festivities, was the lovely woman from Dallas that I had been dating at the time I met with Albert. She later married an American diplomat assigned to help Russia achieve its economic goals. They were both now living in the former Soviet Union. I googled her and saw that she had even written a book about their experiences. It was entitled *RUSSIAN LESSONS.* I am assuming Albert picked up her vibe from me. That is impressive. At any rate, I decided to follow his advice. Rather than take any other PR job, I made a gutsy decision for me. I up and moved to Chicago for two years. The woman whose vibration Albert had sensed had been transferred from Dallas to Chicago. One night while we were conversing long distance, she invited me to come and stay with her for a few weeks. It sounded good to me. I was footloose and fancy free. In no time at all, I was driving north for an adventure. And what an adventure it turned out to be. It represented a crucial step forward on my spiritual journey.

I am going to leave my story at this point. This book is about your company and finding its spiritual purpose. What I would like to communicate through my own personal experience is this: stay open to taking the uncommon path. You may discover unexpected revelations that could take your organization to new levels of success and satisfaction.

I close the narrative of my transition from the corporate world to the ministry with one final story. On October 25, 1990, I was in Missouri to receive my diploma as a graduate of Unity's Continuing Education Program (CEP). This was the preparational study for the Ministerial Education Program (MEP), from which I graduated and was ordained two years later. On the very day that I received my diploma as a CEP graduate, the business section of *The Kansas City Star* displayed this top-of-the-fold shocking headline:

THE SOUTHLAND CORPORATION

DECLARES BANKRUPTCY

But that must be a story for another time. Today, 7-Eleven has reconstituted itself as a successful international corporation with 71,100 stores throughout the world. It is owned by Seven & I Holdings, a descendant of our original Japanese licensee Ito-Yokado. "Oh, Thank Heaven for 7-Eleven" is still used occasionally as an advertising theme. I am proud of my service with the little ice company in Dallas that grew up to serve the world.

15

The Social Media Graveyard

I earned My PR chops long before the advent of social media. So please take these thoughts for what they are worth and leave the rest. I see SM as a potential graveyard for some unsuspecting companies. You need to know the stakes involved should your company become a target from those who patrol various online platforms. First, let me say something that may strike you as paradoxical: not all SM criticism is bad. In fact, your company might even gain some perspective by finding yourself in the online crosshairs. Should it happen to the organization you represent, ask yourself these three questions: (1) Is what our critics say true? (2) Is our reputation in real jeopardy? And (3) what realistically can we do to defend our company? There is one thing you can do now, before the flaming arrows start flying. Think seriously about creating a Social Media Active Response Team (SMART). I feel quite certain many forward-thinking companies have already taken this step. If you have not done so, I would suggest you identify your sharpest tech employees. Seek out those who thoroughly understand SM. Consider forming an ad hoc committee that can be summoned together to address fast rising issues. This is not a PR area in which to take chances. The internet's impact is immediate and unforgiving. Be prepared for anything. I can almost guarantee the problems will arise from an unexpected source. Review your products and services for vulnerabilities. Strange things could and probably will happen. If they do, you are ready with your SMART group. If it never happens, God has blessed you in a special way.

Final Thoughts About Helping Your Company Find Its Spiritual Purpose

I feel strongly about the power of a company or corporation to change our society and world for the better. I have seen it happen. However, we live in an era of big government. The prevailing wisdom says that it takes federal and state governments to make the huge changes necessary to improve lives and solve big problems. To some degree, that will always be true. However, I also believe the corporate world possesses distinct advantages over the government bureaucracy: (1) Companies can make decisions faster and then move quickly to implement those decisions; they can take positive actions to affect change while the government is still in the legislative, research and development phase; (2) Although there are many talented people in government; in general, the more creative types choose either the entrepreneurial or corporate path; i. e. Steve Jobs, Bill Gates or Elon Musk probably would not do well as GS-15s; (3) A preoccupation with spirituality is not something I equate with government, plus there is a reason why our founders wanted to separate church and state; (4) Companies in many ways are more tuned in to real people than a distant and enormous central government; if something is not working, a corporation will know about it quicker through both employee and customer feedback; However, I will acknowledge government is getting better in some cases (I love the VA now) but there is still that ever-present bureaucratic mind-set that places caution and safety above risk-taking and (5) I believe the best companies lead from the heart; In some cases, that can also be said for government as well. I do believe the next great idea to lift humankind will come, not from government or even a religious entity. It will originate with a company or corporation. God has many brilliant divine ideas floating around in the ethers. Who knows? Maybe one of those creative new ideas will come from you and/or the great people around you. Perhaps a "Cause" will emerge that changes your company and maybe even the world. I am putting my money on you—and God--to produce the miracles we need.

P. S. ONE MORE BIG IDEA

Allow me to leave you with one more Big Idea for your possible spiritual purpose. I believe there are three major areas that hold significant promise for corporate involvement in the challenging years that lie ahead:

BODY

MIND

SPIRIT

There are numerous areas in each of these categories that offer great potential for companies to get involved.

BODY—Hunger is still a major problem in this country. The Feeding America people (www.feedingamerica.org) have already collected several important corporate and other sponsors. You may have seen the Subaru commercials for Feeding Hunger on national TV. The "Body" aspect of this "purpose" possibility also includes the fast-growing field of nutrition. it is not just having enough to eat. It also means putting healthy food into our bodies. Taking care of our physical body includes exercise and keeping harmful substances away from it. When we pollute and disrespect our God-given body temple, a lifetime of health problems can be triggered. Being overweight in America is a related challenge. That can tie in to both the exercise and nutritional opportunities for a healthier nation.

MIND—Mental health is another problem that requires everyone's attention. Keeping the human mind pure and healthy is a lifelong challenge. I believe corporate involvement in the mental health area could raise awareness and help generate solutions. As we age, this urgent problem will become an even greater necessity to address. Alzheimer and dementia research must keep advancing. However, I think we need to pay attention to all ages and genders for signs of cognitive decline. Drug and alcohol abuse will always be with us. That scourge has already led to huge societal problems. We need to find new ways to keep people's minds active and engaged in healthy pursuits. It is just my opinion, but constantly watching crime shows on TV does not seem like a positive use of anybody's time. Spending thousands of hours viewing human beings harm each other uplifts no one. If we do not address mental health issues, unthinkable actions (such as mass shootings) are likely to continue destabilizing our nation. I

believe we are facing a mental health emer-
gency. We must address it.

SPIRIT—Our inner spirit needs constant comfort, hope and encouragement. I believe people
are basically good. We care about each other.
But our gentle spirits are vulnerable flowers
that need regular watering. For example, introducing the healing properties of meditation to
all ages could have a calming effect on society. I
also support anything that nurtures our spiritual lives. Twelve step programs such as Alcoholics Anonymous, Narcotics Anonymous and
Al-Anon Family Groups are powerful supple-
ments for our inner lives. Personally, I would
also support more reading of the Holy Bible and
increased study of God's Word in general. God
placed so much wisdom, comfort and support in
these pages. The stories and people of The Bible
are relevant to today.

I hope you will consider programs in the body,
mind and spirit areas. There remains so much
that you and your company can do to heal and
change the world. One company, one person and
one big idea is enough to lift the earth to a new
consciousness. This possibility may indeed fall
to you and your organization.

I will close with a story of what occurred on a
normal business trip in January of 1968. I was
in Miami for a meeting with Russ Nicoll, our
Velda Farms sales manager. One of our big
Southland dairy accounts was the plush Four
Seasons Hotel, so Russ had gotten me a room

there. As I was strolling the hotel lobby headed for breakfast one morning, I saw two distinguished African American gentlemen coming toward me. They both looked familiar. As we came face to face, I recognized Dr. Martin Luther King, Jr. and Ralph Abernathy. I believe they were staying at the hotel for a meeting of the Southern Christian Leadership Conference. I recall that we passed with a smile and a nod of the head from Dr. King. How I wished I had just thanked him during those few precious seconds for changing the world. Never underestimate the power of one person with a spiritual purpose.

THE END

A Personal Thank You

There are so many Southland Corporation and
7-Eleven people who made our PR programs
successful. I must recognize their contributions,
although I am sure somebody will be left out.
From Southland management, I salute the
Thompson family (John, Jere and Jodie III),
Clark Matthews II, the late Dick Dole, Mr.
Hartfelder, (as in Herbert E.) , W. K. Ruppen-
kamp, Walton Grayson III, Clifford Wheeler,
Vaughn Heady and Forrest Stout from the
Stores Group, Jim Parker, M. T. (Tom) Cochran,
Jr. and Tex Beshears from the Southland Dair-
ies Group, great 7-Eleven division and zone
managers like Mitch Telson, Don Barfield, Bob
Sally, Don Burnside, Ben Hund, Jack Dold and
Ben Holland; stores marketing whizzes like Bob
Gallana, Dick Turchi, Billy Ruffeno, Dennis
Potts, John Pearman, Ken Davis and G. Alan
Williams; Velda Farms sales manager Russ
Nicoll; the three amigos from Midwest Farms:
Jack Gentle, Nick Douzanis and Tom Hill; PR
department stalwarts like Jean Muller, the late

Dan McCurdy, Eric Norrington, Alisa Martin, Pat Pape, Jim Shaughnessy, Karen Raskopf, Margaret Chabris, Janey Appia, Bob Schiers, Cheryl Bayse, Jean Thompson and Markeeta McNatt, the Andrews' sisters Shirley (my secretary) and Sheila (Walton Grayson III's secretary), designers Hans Streich and Dee Ann Steiger; Stanford Agency geniuses Howard W. Greene, Dick Boone, Bob Peck, Neil Ledyard, Jack Dwyer, Gary Bradbury, Don Coburn, Mark James, Steve Patterson, Ken Heckmann, Doug Reynolds ,Susan Kendall, Bill Scott and the one and only Frank Harting; and outside PR consultants Mike Sunshine, Martin Janis, Karl Yehle, Roy Leffingwell, Joe McCarthy, Marty Cooper, Kay Berger, and Woody Kepner. I also want to mention one of the smartest people in the company: the late Effie Carter from the 11th floor. Everybody paid attention to your wise opinion.

About The Author

Rev. Allen C. Liles is a graduate of Baylor University in Waco, TX and the Unity School of Religious Studies in Unity Village, MO. Prior to entering the ministry, he served as vice president, public relations for The Southland Corporation in Dallas, TX and communications manager for The McLane Company in Temple, TX. Rev. Liles was also senior director for Outreach at Unity Village from 1995-2001. He has served as senior minister at Unity churches in Missouri, Arizona and Minnesota.

BOOKS BY ALLEN C. LILES

Exodus 20/The Ten Commandments

Ephesians 6/ Putting On the Full Armor of God

John 14/The Most Important Chapter in the New Testament

Sitting With God/Meditating For God's Divine Guidance

The 7 Puzzles of Life/God's Plan to Save the World

The Forever Penny/ How Our Loved Ones Stay Connected After Death

Oh Thank Heaven/The Story of the Southland Corporation

E-books:
The 12 Promises of Heaven/
http://smashwords.com/books/view/444920

Friends of Jesus/
http://smashwords.com/books/view/455617

E-Spiritual Rehab/
http://smashwords.com/books/view/481978

The Book of Celeste/
http://smashwords.com/books/view/593856

The Book of Floyd/
http://smashwords.com/books/view/615914

The Book of Ethan/
http://smashwords.com/books/view/647665

Audio/CD
The Peaceful Driver/Steering Clear of Road Rage/Unity